General Directions

Anatomy of Neckties

Silk is the natural fiber used most in fashion ties. The silk may be woven with different-colored threads to produce the design of the tie, or the design may be printed directly onto the fabric. You will also find cotton and wool ties, but they are produced in small quantities. Synthetic materials are used in the majority of ties currently manufactured. Polyester is the leading synthetic used along with acetate, rayon, and nylon.

Quality men's ties are cut on the bias grain of the cloth so they will knot properly. Two or three pieces of the fabric are sewn into the "envelope" containing the interlining. The wool or wool blend interlining gives the ties consistency and shape. The "tipping" fabric is acetate or silk sewn onto the back of both ends of a tie forming a lining.

The label is another small piece of fabric sewn to the back of the tie, usually about seven inches from the tip. The label may name the fiber used, and/or the maker of the tie.

Ties can be used in their basic shape, or they can be cut and used as fabric yardage.

Preparing the Ties

Remove the label by using a seam ripper to break the thread tacks. Then remove the interlining and lining by pulling the thread from the wide end of the tie. The first stitching can usually be removed easily. Use a small pair of scissors or a seam ripper to aid in opening the seam. Remove the interlining fabric. The lining of the wide end is usually stitched with an overlock chain stitch and can be unraveled from each side to the point. Use the same procedure to remove the lining from the narrow end.

If you only need small pieces, you may remove the linings more quickly by using a rotary cutter to cut away the fold lines along each length of the tie. Some of the tie fabric will be wasted but time will be saved.

Cleaning the Ties

You may gently wash most ties. If you want the finished quilt to be washable, wash all of the ties being used in that quilt. Use warm water and a gentle washing product such as Orvus and wash the ties by hand in a sink. Rinse thoroughly and then smooth the ties out flat on a towel to dry.

If you do not want your finished quilt to be washable, the ties can be processed by a commercial dry cleaner or done in a laundromat dry cleaner. Several pounds can easily be done in this manner, but remove the lining and interlining first.

If you dry clean the ties, be sure to label the quilt for dry cleaning later.

Press the ties. Use a moderately warm iron and steam. If using the ties in the original shape, fold on the original creases and press. If using as fabric, press each tie out flat.

Sorting the Ties

Select ties to use in your quilt the same way you choose other fabrics for quilts. Consider the colors, the design motifs, and the scale of the designs. The final look of the tie is so important that the design motif may determine the weave, the printing, and the manufacturing process.

All-over designs repeat design motifs such as small geometric shapes, polka dots, animals, or fleur-de-lis. Ties with larger motifs have the look of upholstery fabric. Most tie collections will include geometrics, stripes, polka dots, plaids, and paisley designs. Figurative motifs found on ties include animals, sports and hunting themes, plants and humorous art. The width of the tie determines the scale of the motif with some of the wider ties having very bold designs and color schemes.

You may choose to use only one type of fabric in your quilt, or you may mix the polyester, silk, and ties made from blends of fibers. Select additional yardage for the sashings, borders and binding from compatible fibers.

Techniques for Sewing

The following special techniques for piecing quilts are very helpful when using the fabrics from men's ties.

Rotary Cutting

Use rotary cutter, mat, and acrylic ruler to measure and cut pieces including seam allowance. The directions for each quilt will give the sizes of the pieces you will need.

Template Piecing

Make plastic templates from the pattern pieces for your quilt.

If you are piecing by hand, trace pattern onto template plastic along inner dashed line, **Fig 1**; cut out. Trace template onto wrong side of tie fabric; cut fabric 1/4" beyond traced line. Match traced lines when stitching pieces together by placing pin directly in corners, **Fig 2**.

If you are machine piecing, trace pattern piece onto template plastic along outer solid line, **Fig 3**; cut out. Trace template onto wrong side of tie fabric; cut fabric along traced line. Sew pieces together using a 1/4" seam allowance.

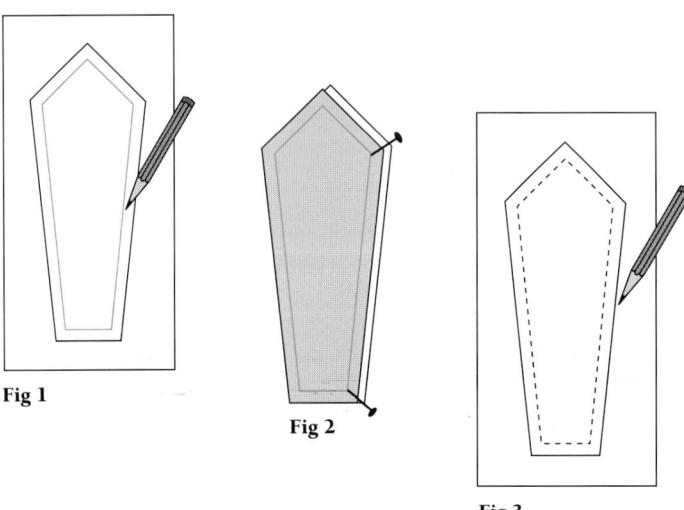

Fig 1

Fig 2

Fig 3

Paper Piecing

Use a precut paper shape for the repeating pieces of a quilt block. Commercially cut and packaged papers are available for patchwork in squares, triangles, diamonds (both 45° and 60°), hexagons and half hexagons, and for appliqué in hearts and Dresden plates. You can also cut multiple shapes from light-weight paper using scissors or rotary cutter. Cut out along inner dashed line.

Pin paper shape to wrong side of fabric. Cut the fabric, allowing 1/4" for seams, **Fig 4**. Fold seam allowance over the paper and hand baste, **Fig 5**, placing knotted thread end on right side of the fabric so it will be easy to remove after sewing pieces together.

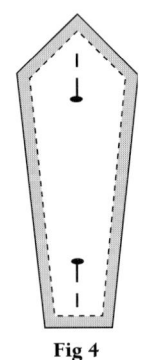
Fig 4

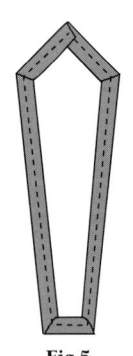
Fig 5

Join pieces by placing right sides together and stitching with small whip stitches just catching the edges of the fabric, **Fig 6**.

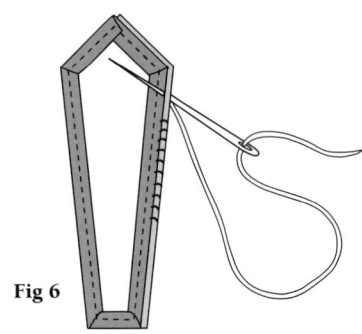

Fig 6

When all pieces are joined, open block flat and press lightly. Remove basting threads and paper shapes. Press again.

Foundation Paper Piecing for Crazy Quilts

Sewing pieces of fabric on a paper foundation is a traditional method of quiltmaking which insures accuracy in piecing. Choose a paper that is easy to remove. (Use typing paper, computer paper, copy paper or just about any inexpensive paper.)

1. Cut paper in the shape desired (squares, triangles, diamonds, etc.).

2. Place one piece of fabric right side up at center of paper foundation, **Fig 7**.

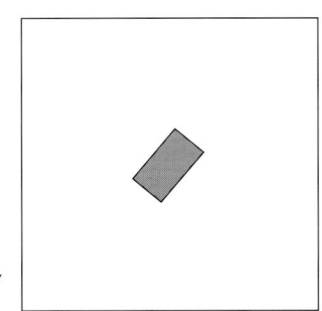

Fig 7

3. Add a second piece of fabric right sides together with the one in place; stitch a 1/4" seam, **Fig 8**. Trim any excess fabric. Fold the second piece open; press, **Fig 9**.

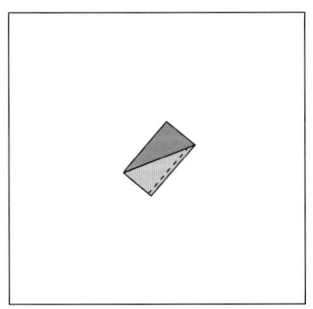

Fig 8

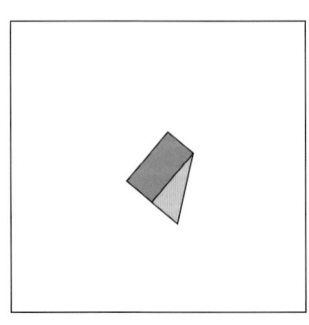

Fig 9

4. Keep adding fabric pieces one at a time to center piece until entire foundation is covered, **Fig 10**. Press carefully after each seam so piece remains flat.

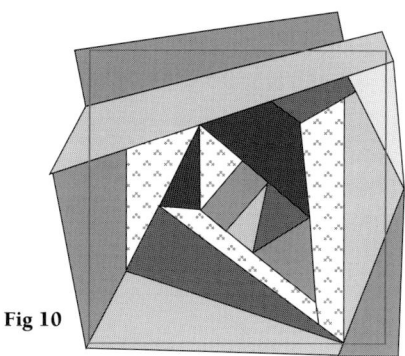

Fig 10

5. Trim fabric along edge of paper shape. Remove paper.

Foundation Fabric Piecing

Traditionally quilts made using fabric foundations include early Log Cabin and Pineapple patterns as well as traditional crazy quilts.

1. Cut squares of muslin or other lightweight, solid fabric.

2. Draw and number design on muslin, **Fig 11**. (*Example shows a Log Cabin block.*)

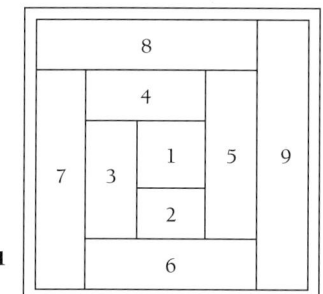

Fig 11

3. Place first fabric right side up on **unmarked** side of muslin making sure it overlaps all sides of first marked space, **Fig 12**. Place second fabric right sides together with first, **Fig 13**; pin in place.

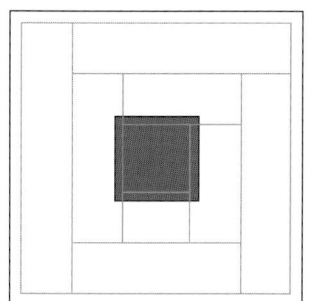

Fig 12

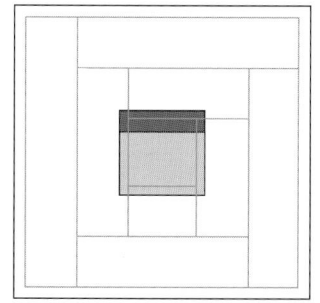

Fig 13

4. Turn piece over to **marked** side and stitch first seam between #1 and #2 as marked on muslin, **Fig 14**. Press fabric open, **Fig 15**.

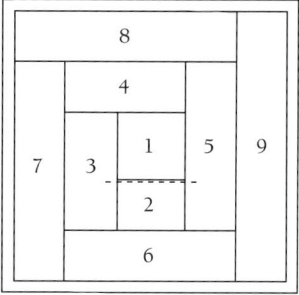

Fig 14

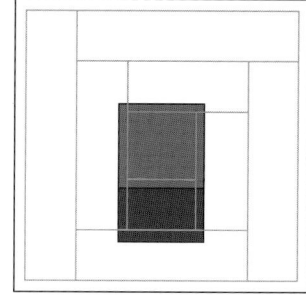

Fig 15

5. Continue in numerical order, pressing carefully after each addition.

Freezer Paper Piecing

Many tie fabrics are "creepy" and "wiggly" and difficult to cut and sew. Use freezer paper to stabilize the fabric.

1. Trace pattern pieces along inner dashed line on paper side of freezer paper. Cut apart with paper scissors (do not use your good fabric scissors)

2. Press freezer paper templates with shiny side against wrong side of tie fabric with an iron. Heat setting should be suitable for your fabric.

3. Cut out shapes allowing 1/4" seam, **Fig 16**.

4. Pin pieces to be sewn at corners and along edges of freezer paper.

5. Stitch along edge of freezer paper, **Fig 17**.

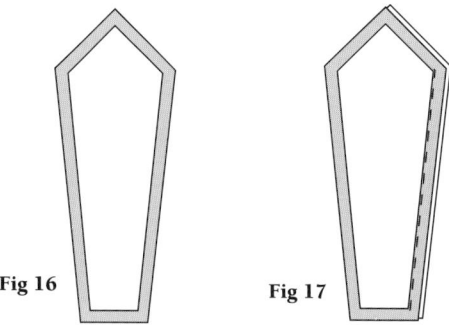

Fig 16   Fig 17

6. When block is completed and joined in setting, remove freezer paper.

Interfacing

You may stabilize the tie fabric by using a thin fusible interfacing. This will add too much bulk if you are hand quilting, but the extra is workable if you plan to tie or machine quilt.

Finishing the Quilt

Setting Blocks with Lattice Strips

Lattice strips are used in both straight and diagonal settings to frame the blocks and to enlarge the overall size of the quilt. A bit of early measuring and marking will insure that the strips line up straight, making the quilt top flat.

First, sew the small lattice strips to the blocks forming rows, **Fig 1**. When you have cut the long strips that go between the rows, mark the fabric in the following order: 1/4" seam allowance, finished block size, finished lattice size, finished block size, finished lattice size, and so forth until ending with a finished block size and a 1/4" seam allowance, **Fig 2**. Mark on both edges of the strip. Pin the strip to the row, matching the seams in the rows to the marks on the strips, **Fig 3**. This will evenly align all the rows across the quilt and prevent extra fabric being "ruffled" into the strips.

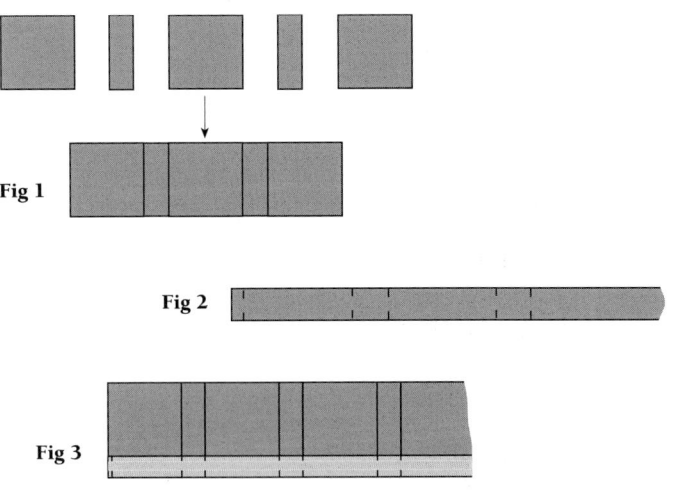

How to Add Borders (not Ruffles)

Borders that lay flat with smooth corners are easy to achieve with some careful measuring.

After the blocks have been set, fold the bottom of the quilt up to the top and to see if they are the same. Fold the quilt in half lengthwise and see if the sides are the same length. Minor differences can be accommodated, but if you have big differences, check to see why and correct by adjusting seams in the setting strips.

Measure the length of the quilt on the center fold. Cut side borders to that measurement, adding a couple inches for insurance. (It is easy to cut this off later, but a nuisance to piece on 3/4" if there is a problem!)

Measure width of quilt including borders along center fold. Cut top and bottom borders to this measurement, again adding a couple inches for insurance.

Mark center of each edge of the quilt with a pin. Starting with sides, fold top portion of quilt toward center; place a pin at the fold for a quarter measure. Fold again, pin to pin, and mark eighths. Repeat with lower portion of quilt, **Fig 4**. Mark top and bottom edges of quilt top in quarters using the same method, folding sides of quilt toward center, **Fig 5**.

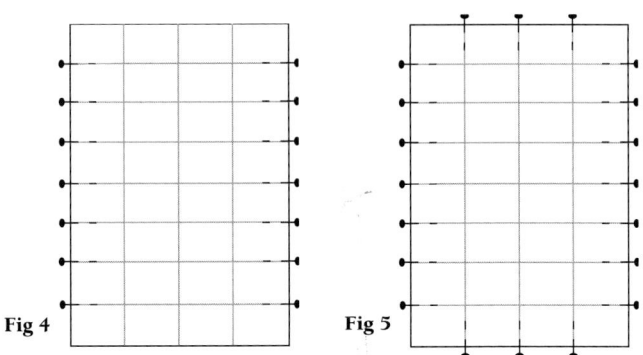

Mark center of each border piece with a pin. Then, mark the inches of the measurements between pins in quilt top, leaving the "insurance inches" at each end, **Fig 6**.

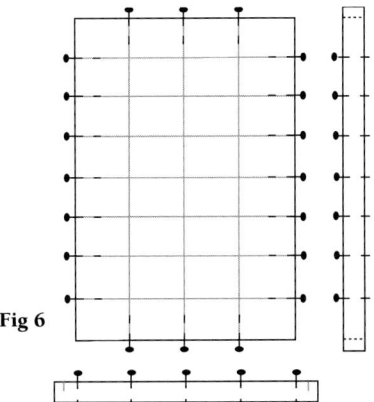

Beginning with side borders first, pin border strip to quilt at center, quarters, eighths, and then as often as you need in order to stitch without stretching the border. If there is a slight difference in the border measurements, "ease" the extra fabric in equally over the length of the border. Sew in place. Repeat for top and bottom borders.

Quilting Designs

Where to put quilting stitches depends somewhat on the design of the quilt. You can outline basic design elements or areas defined by a different color. Quilting designs have been suggested for several of the quilts pictured.

Always test the marker you plan to use for marking the quilting designs. Chalk markers that brush off can be used for simple grids and straight lines. Mark a block at a time, as the chalk does not handle well. Wash-off markers require water on the quilt, so be sure you have pre-washed all the materials and ties used.

You might like to try freezer paper designs that can be pressed on the quilt with a warm iron. After quilting the design, gently lift the paper off.

How to Layer Lining, Batting and Quilt Top

Press the quilt top after the final border has been added. Look on the wrong side and re-press any seam allowances that have been pressed incorrectly. Measure the width and length.

Cut and seam the lining fabric, allowing four inches in extra width and length (two inches all around the quilt top).

Tumble the polyester batting in a warm dryer to "relax" the fold lines from packaging.

Place lining, wrong side up, on a large table or clean carpet. Tape or pin the lining taut; keep corners square. Spread batting over lining; trim batting to same size as lining. Center quilt top on batting and lining. Starting at center of the quilt, pin all three layers together with one-inch safety pins; work out from center, pinning about every eight inches. Loosen tape, or edge pins. Fold lining over batting and pin to "seal" the edge.

Quilt according to the designs you have chosen, beginning in the center of the quilt. Continue to enlarge the quilted area from the center out. Work to make your stitches even, not just small.

Tying Quilts

Many of the quilts in this book are tied rather than quilted. Use yarn, embroidery floss, perle cotton or narrow ribbon for the ties and a needle with an eye large enough to hold the thread.

Once the quilt top is layered with batting and lining and basted, begin tying. With needle threaded, go into the quilt from the top all the way through to the back; come back up through quilt about 1/8" to 1/4" from where needle first entered. Tie ends in a square knot; trim ends. If desired, make a small bow before trimming ends. Repeat at least every 6", closer if quilt is to be washed frequently.

How to Make Bias Binding

The following instructions for continuous Bias Cut with Rotary Cutter are from Jackie Reis of Accu-Patterns.

Making the Continuous Bias Strip

When over one yard (in length) of bias edging is needed, use a calculator and the following method to determine the size of the square needed.

1. Find the distance, in inches, around the quilt: two lengths plus two widths.

2. Add 10" for mitering corners and overlap.

3. Multiply this number by the width of the binding you plan to cut.

4. Push the "square root" symbol on the calculator. Round to the next highest whole number and add the width of the binding you plan to cut. This is the size of the square required.

Example: The quilt measures 92" x 110"

   1. 92 + 110 = 202 (length plus width)
      202 x 2 = 404 (distance around quilt)
   2. 404 + 10 = 414 (perimeter plus allowance)
   3. 414 x 2 (width to cut binding) = 828
   4. square root of 828 = 28.7749 round to 29 and
      2 = 31" square required

Once you have the size of the square that you need, cut it in half diagonally, **Fig 7**. Place pieces, right sides together, to form a "giant tooth;" off-set edges, then sew together by machine using a 3/8" seam allowance, **Fig 8**. Press seam open.

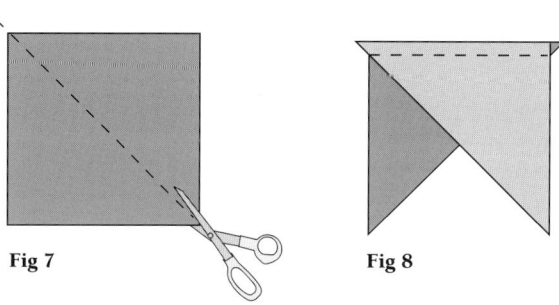

Fig 7   Fig 8

Place fabric on cutting board with wrong side of fabric touching the board and bias edges parallel to the length of the board, **Fig 9**.

Fold upper tip of fabric down to seam line, **Fig 10**; fold lower tip up to seam line so the straight grain edges meet diagonally, but do not overlap at this butting line.

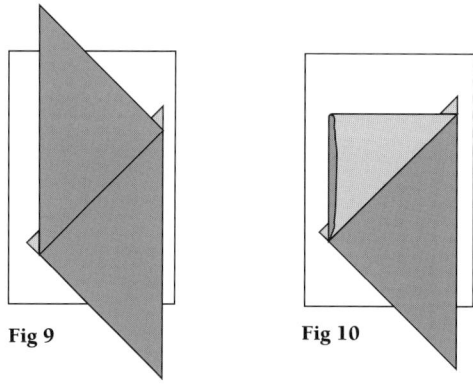

Fig 9   Fig 10

Keep bias edges even on left side and as even as possible on the right. (Left-handed users, reverse these directions.) Fabric will be two thicknesses. Begin cutting the width desired from the left (lefties on the right) using rotary cutter, mat, and acrylic ruler. The cut will "jump across" the butting line; that is, stop the cutting 1" before the line and start again 1" after the line. Continue to cut across the width of the fabric with parallel cuts, jumping across the butting line on each cut. Cut through and discard the last incomplete row, **Fig 11**.

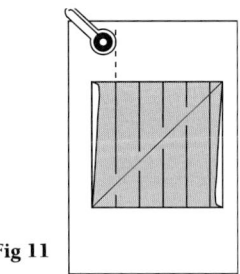

Fig 11

Referring to **Fig 12**, gently lift up the tip of the first row and use scissors to cut through to the end of fabric (see A+); gently lift up the top of the last row and cut through to the end of fabric (see B).

Gently slide and align the fabrics at the butting line so that A is even with A+ and B is even with B+, **Fig 13**. With right sides together, join butted edges together with a 3/8" seam allowance forming a tube.

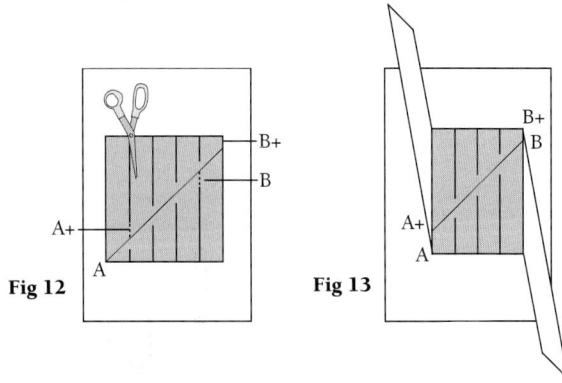

Fig 12   Fig 13

Slide the fabric tube over the ironing board; press seam open. Using a good pair of fabric scissors, cut across uncut portions of fabric making a long, continuous strip, **Fig 14**. Unwind bias strip from board.

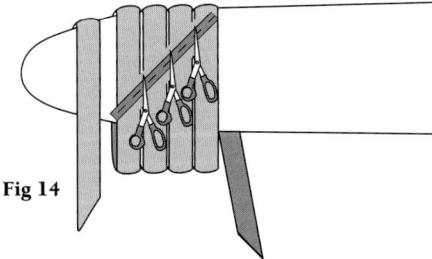

Fig 14

If you are making a doubled binding, press strip in half lengthwise with wrong sides together.

Sewing Binding to Quilt (for Mitered Corners)

Leaving a 6" to 8" tail, place binding right sides together with layered quilt (quilt top, batting and lining) along raw edge; sew binding to quilt, using a 1/4" seam allowance, to within 8" from a corner. If necessary, adjust distance to avoid having a binding seam fall at the corner.

Continue to stitch binding to within 1/4" from edge of quilt top, **Fig 15**. (If you are using a larger seam allowance, you will stop at that distance from edge.) Backstitch to anchor.

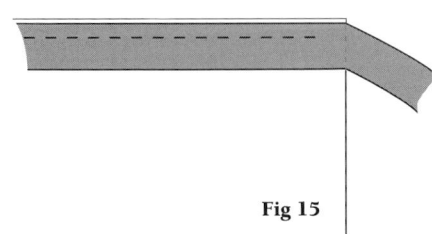

Fig 15

Fold binding to back of quilt and finger crease binding at fold, **Fig 16**. Bring the creased fold to the top of the quilt corner and begin stitching where previous stitching stopped, **Fig 17**; backstitch to anchor.

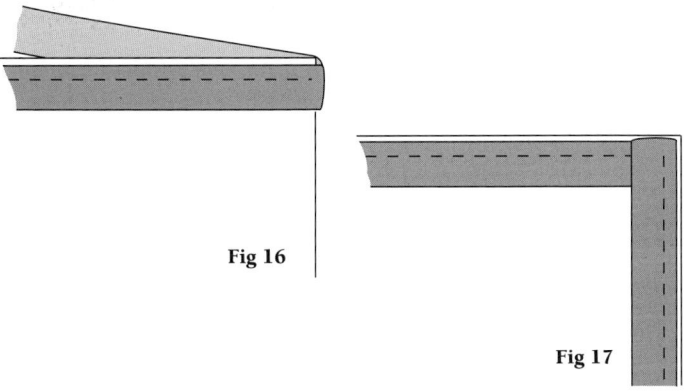

Fig 16   Fig 17

As you approach a corner and find that a seam will fall in the corner miter, cut off the binding in a diagonal cut two or three inches before the corner turn. Rejoin bias strip in a diagonal seam and continue sewing bias to quilt, turning remaining corners in same manner.

Final Joining of Binding in a Diagonal Seam

Stop stitching about 8" from beginning stitching. Tails should overlap several inches. Insert a straight pin into the quilt in the middle of the joining space, **Fig 18**.

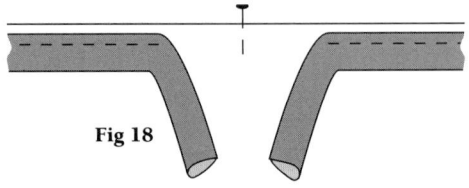

Fig 18

Pin strips together, but not to quilt, at the point where the pin is in the quilt. Binding should fit comfortably along unsewn edge. Remove pin in quilt, **Fig 19**.

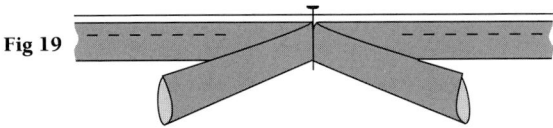

Fig 19

Measuring from the binding pin, cut the strips 1/2 the width of the binding. (If binding is cut 2", each strip is cut 1" from the pin, **Fig 20**.)

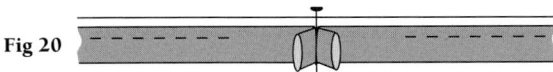

Fig 20

Remove binding pin, open left strip wrong side up (A), open right strip right side up (B), **Fig 21**. Place end A at right angle to, and on top of end B, **Fig 22**; pin. Stitch diagonally across the joining to form a triangle, **Fig 23**.

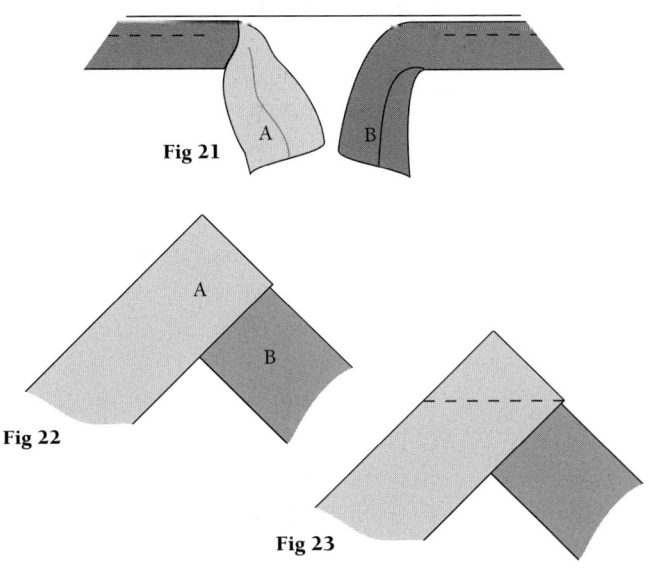

Fig 21

A

B

Fig 22

Fig 23

Open binding; refold on fold line if using a doubled binding. The distance of the unsewn binding should match the unsewn distance of the quilt. Trim off excess triangle of seam allowance, **Fig 24**; finger press seam open and stitch to quilt.

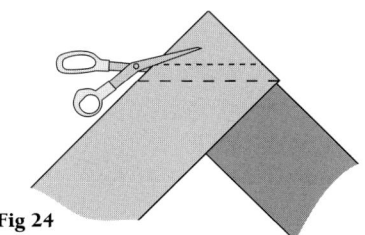

Fig 24

Finishing the Binding

Using thread to match binding, hand stitch binding to quilt back, covering the seam line.

At corners, use thumb nail to encourage miter on front of quilt. Fold binding up and over toward back of quilt, **Fig 25**. For the ultimate look, sew miters closed on front and back, **Fig 26**.

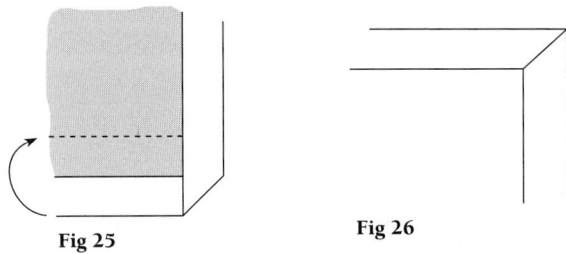

Fig 25

Fig 26

How to Sign and Date Your Tie Quilt

Signing the quilt can be a simple matter of writing your name with a permanent fabric pen (see note below), or an elaborate cross stitch project, embellished with embroidery.

Include the name of the quiltmaker (add your maiden name; it will soon be forgotten otherwise), the date the quilt was finished, and the city and state where the quiltmaker lives. Use the label to tell about the ties in the quilt. Some of the quilts in this book included tie labels stitched to the backs.

Note: *Pigma™ fine point pens don't bleed when used on fabric. Iron a square of muslin on a piece of freezer paper to stabilize fabric for ease in writing. Practice writing slowly. Be sure to remove the paper before stitching the label onto back of quilt.*

Retired Ties

Donna Phillips of Lubbock, Texas, designed this wall quilt in 1986. This was the first quilt she ever designed. Donna combined cotton quilt fabrics with pieces from the neckties. She used several different patterns in several sizes in a strip setting.

Wall Quilt: 27 1/2" x 39"

Fabric Requirements:

Note: Refer to color photograph, page 23, and Quilt Layout, page 11, when deciding which ties to use so that you can use them to your best advantage. Fabric colors are given in the Cutting List as a guide to placement in the photographed quilt. Choose your own scraps of coordinating cotton fabrics to complement your own special ties.

12 to 15 assorted ties
several 1/4 yd scraps coordinating cotton fabrics (If a suitable color or pattern is not available in your ties, use a scrap of solid or print fabric.)
1 1/4 yds solid black, lining
1/2 yd red print, sashing and binding
batting

Pattern Pieces:

A Small Triangle
B Medium Triangle
C Half Circle
D Medium Circle
E Small Circle
F Heart

Cutting List:

Star Block
eight A Small Triangles, blue print tie
eight A Small Triangles, red solid
four 2" squares, red solid
one 3 1/2" square, blue print tie

Medium Circle Block
one D Medium Circle, blue print tie
one D Medium Circle, blue gray print tie
two 3 1/2" x 12 3/4" strips, dk blue tie

Diagonal Stripe Block
one 1 1/2" x 3" strip, lt gray solid
one 1 1/2" x 5" strip, dk red solid
one 1 1/2" x 7" strip, dk gray solid
one 1 1/2" x 9" strip, med red solid
one 1 1/2" x 11" strip, teal solid
one 1 1/2" x 11" strip, lt gray solid
one 1 1/2" x 8 1/4" strip, dk red solid
one 1 1/2" x 6 1/4" strip, dk gray solid

Shown in color on page 23

one 1 1/2" x 4" strip, med red solid
one 1 1/2" x 2" strip, teal solid
Prairie Point Block
four 3 3/4" squares, gray print tie
one 6 1/2" x 8 1/4" rectangle, teal solid
Half Circle Block
one C Half Circle, blue print tie
one 7 3/4" x 12 3/4" rectangle, black solid
Pieced Strip
seven 1 1/2" x 2" strips, assorted solids
Heart Block
one F Heart, red solid
one 4" x 5" rectangle, black solid
one 3" x 20 3/4" strip, black stripe tie
one 5" x 20 3/4" strip, black/white polka dot tie
Flying Geese
36 A Small Triangles, solid teal
18 B Medium Triangles, assorted ties
Small Circle Block
three E Small Circles, assorted ties
one 5 1/2" x 12" rectangle, red solid
Diagonal Tie Block
assorted tie strips at least 10" long
one 2" x 19 1/4" strip, dk blue print
Additional Pieces
one 2 1/4" x 6 1/2" strip, blue print tie
one 6 1/2" x 4 1/4" rectangle, pink/red print
one 5" x 7 3/4" rectangle, blue print tie
two 1 1/2" x 27 1/2" strips, red solid
one 9 1/2" square, black/white polka dot cotton
one 1" x 9 1/2" strip, red solid tie
one 2 1/2" x 9 1/2" strip, black stripe tie
one 9 1/2" x 8" rectangle, black print
one 1 1/4" x 9 1/2" strip, red print
one 1 1/4" x 39" strip, red print

Sewing Instructions:

Note: Block construction begins at upper left corner of quilt and continues in vertical rows. Refer to Quilt Layout on page 11.

Star Block

1. Sew med red solid A Small Triangle to blue print A Small Triangle along diagonal edge, **Fig 1**. Repeat for a total of eight pieced squares.

2. Sew pieced triangles together in pairs, **Fig 2**, for a total of four units.

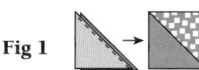
Fig 1

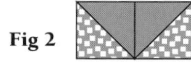
Fig 2

3. Sew a 2" med red solid square to each end of unit, **Fig 3**; repeat one more time.

4. Sew remaining two units to opposite sides of 3 1/2" blue print square, **Fig 4**.

5. Sew rows together to complete Star Block, **Fig 5**.

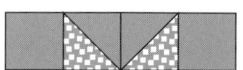
Fig 3

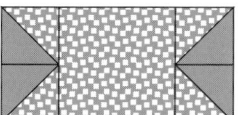
Fig 4

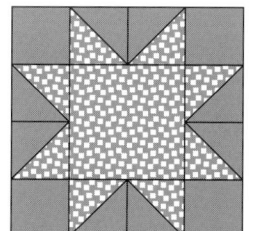
Fig 5

Medium Circle Block

1. Sew two 3 1/2" x 12 3/4" dk blue strips along long edge; press.

2. Turn under edge of blue print D Medium Circle, 1/4"; press. Repeat for other blue print D Medium Circle. Using a blind stitch, appliqué the two Medium Circles centered in rectangle just made, **Fig 6**.

Fig 6

Diagonal Stripe Block

1. Sew 1 1/2"-wide solid strips together as shown in **Fig 7**.

2. Trim block to 6 1/2" x 7 1/2", **Fig 8**.

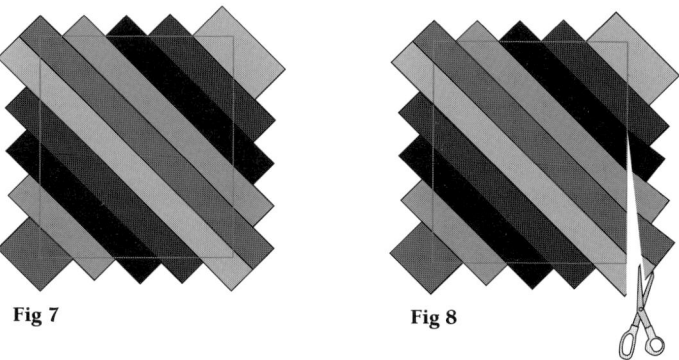
Fig 7   Fig 8

Prairie Point Block

1. Fold 3 3/4" gray print square in half with wrong sides together. Fold each corner at folded edge toward center of opposite side, **Fig 9**; press.

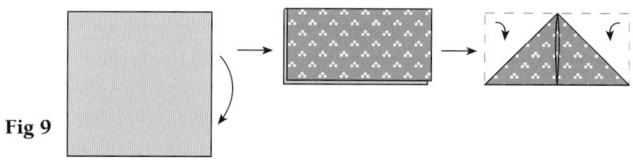
Fig 9

2. Repeat step 1 for a total of four prairie points.

3. Place two prairie points, seam side up, at center of long edges of 6 1/2" x 8 1/4" teal rectangle, **Fig 10**. Baste in place.

Fig 10

Half Circle Block

1. Turn under curved edge of blue print C Half Circle 1/4"; press.

2. Place C Half Circle along one long edge of 7 3/4" x 12 3/4" black rectangle about 2 1/2" from top, **Fig 11**. Using blind stitch, appliqué Half Circle in place along folded curved edge.

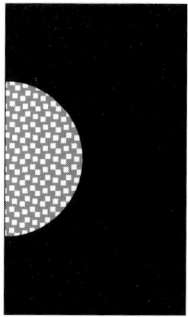
Fig 11

Pieced Strip

1. Sew seven 1 1/2" x 2" assorted strips together along the 2" sides to form strip 2" x 7 1/2", **Fig 12**.

2. Trim strip at both short ends if necessary.

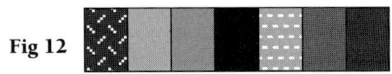

Fig 12

Heart Block

1. Turn under edges of red F Heart 1/4". Place Heart about 5" from top of 5" x 20 3/4" black polka dot strip; blind stitch in place.

2. Sew 3" x 20 3/4" black stripe tie strip to left side of 5" x 20 3/4" black polka dot strip.

3. Turn under 1/4" on one long and one short edge of 4" x 5" black rectangle; place in lower left corner of pieced strips with raw edges even. blind stitch along turned under edges.

Flying Geese

1. Sew diagonal edge of solid teal A Small Triangle to diagonal edge of tie print B Medium Triangle, **Fig 13**; press toward Small Triangle.

2. Sew solid teal A Small Triangle to other diagonal edge of B Medium Triangle to complete Flying Geese Block, **Fig 14**.

Fig 13   Fig 14

3. Repeat steps 1 and 2 for a total of 18 Flying Geese.

4. Referring to Quilt Layout, stitch Flying Geese blocks together with all points in same direction. Sew 1 1/2" x 27 1/2" red solid strip to each long edge.

Small Circles Block

1. Turn under edge of E Small Circle 1/4"; press. Repeat for two remaining E Small Circles.

2. Place Small Circles centered on 5 1/2" x 12" red solid rectangle, **Fig 15**. Using blind stitch, appliqué Small Circles in place.

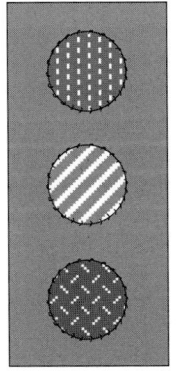

Fig 15

Diagonal Tie Block

1. Piece assorted tie strips diagonally to measure at least 6 1/2" x 19 1/4"; square off to 6 1/2" x 19 1/4".

2. Sew pieced rectangle to right side of 2" x 19 1/4" dk blue print strip.

Finishing

Note: *Blocks are sewn in vertical rows.*

1. For vertical row 1, sew together Star Block, 2 1/4" x 6 1/2" blue print strip, Medium Circle Block, Diagonal Stripe Block, Prairie Point Block and 4 1/4" x 6 1/2" rectangle.

2. For vertical row 2, sew together 5" x 7 3/4" blue print rectangle, Half Circle Block, Pieced Strip and Heart Block.

3. For vertical row 3, sew Flying Geese strip to Small Circles Block.

4. For vertical row 4, sew 9 1/2" polka dot square, 1" x 9 1/2" red strip, 2 1/2" x 9 1/2" black/white stripe strip, 9 1/2" x 8" black rectangle, 1 1/4" x 9 1/2" red print strip and Diagonal Tie Block.

5. Sew vertical rows together in order adding 1 1/4" x 39" red print strip between first and second rows.

6. Mark design for quilting.

7. Layer and baste.

8. Quilt and bind.

9. Sign and date your quilt.

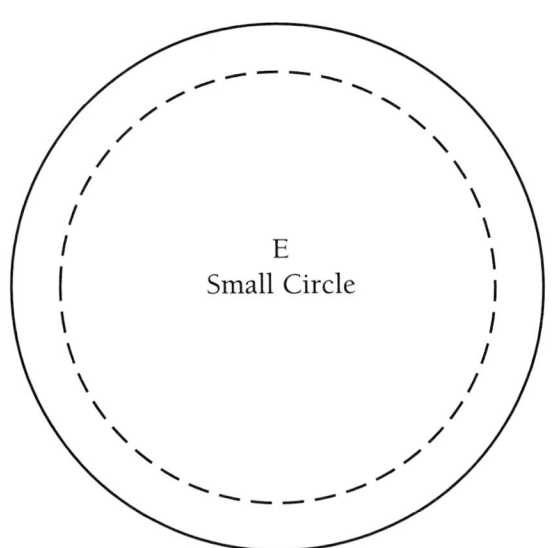

E
Small Circle

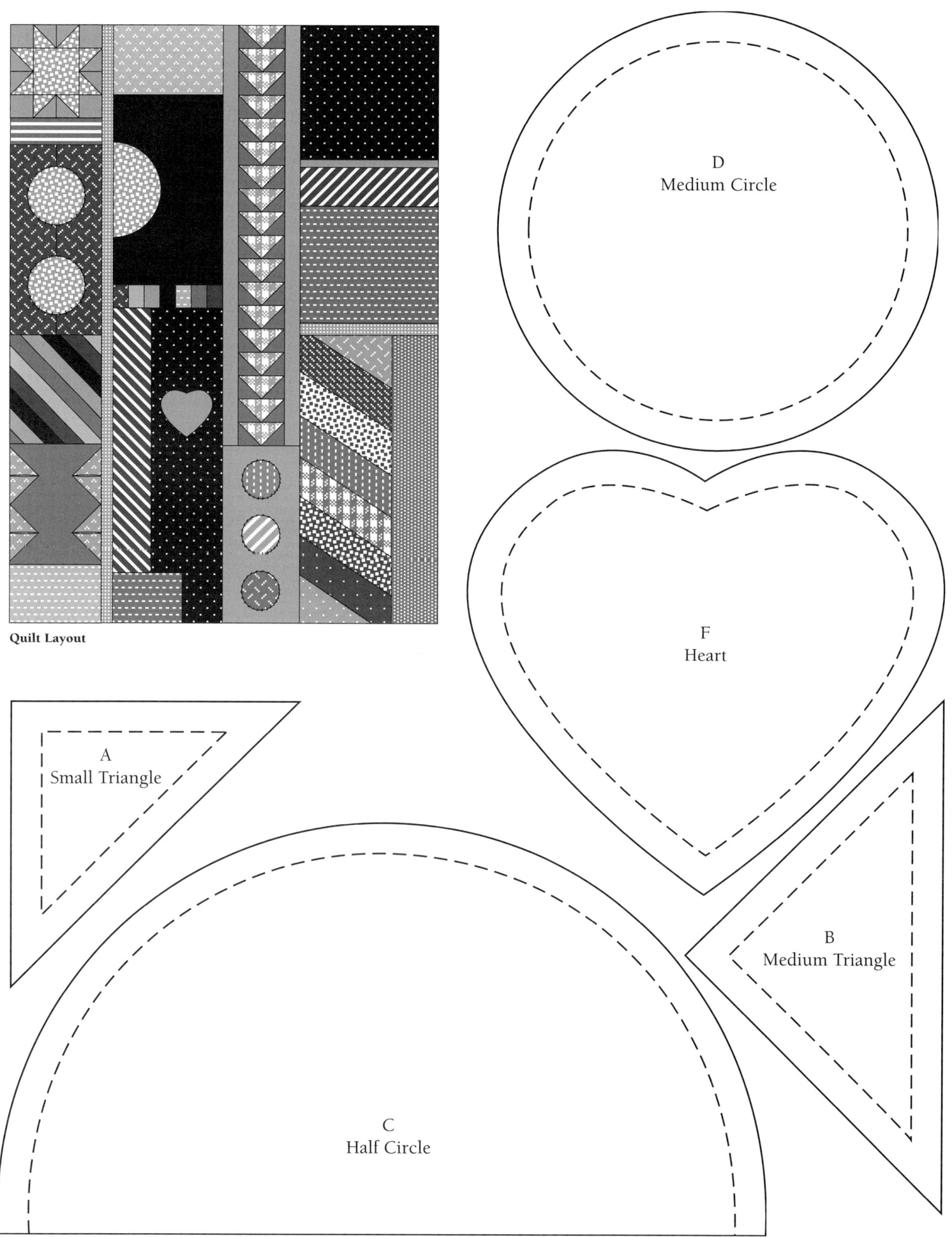

Quilt Layout

D
Medium Circle

F
Heart

A
Small Triangle

B
Medium Triangle

C
Half Circle

11

Fan Fantasy

Lexia Latimer of Meridian, Mississippi had about 300 ties after her husband passed away. This is one of the four quilts she has made for their children using the ties. Lexia is 70 years old.

Queen Size Quilt: 85 1/2" x 99 1/2"

Finished Block Size: 10 1/2"

Fabric Requirements:

30 striped ties for Fan Blades
30 solid color ties for Quarter Circles and border squares
10 print ties for border squares
16 yds off-white fabric for background, lining and binding
batting

Pattern Pieces:

A Full Blade
B Half Blade
C Large Quarter Circle
D Small Quarter Circle
E Background

Cutting List:

30 - 11" x 11" squares, off-white fabric
65 - 3" x 11" lattice strips, off-white fabric
two 5 1/4" x 75 1/2" border strips, off-white fabric
two 5 1/2" x 81" border strips, off-white fabric
66 - 3" x 5 1/2" rectangles, off-white fabric
thirteen 3" x 3" squares, off-white fabric
30 E Background, off-white fabric
150 A Full Blades, striped ties (five per block from same striped ties*)
30 B Half Blades and 30 reversed Half Blades*, striped ties
30 C Large Quarter Circles, solid color ties**
30 D Small Quarter Circles, solid color ties**
140 squares, 3" x 3", assorted ties
* Cut Full Blades, Half Blades and reversed Half Blades from the same striped tie fabric for each block. Position Blades on tie fabric with stripes running through points of Blades, **Fig 1**.
**Cut one Large Quarter Circle and one Small Quarter Circle from each solid color tie.

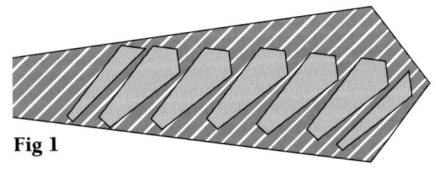

Fig 1

Shown in color on page 22

Sewing Instructions:

Making the Block

1. For one fan, sew five A Full Blades (from the same tie fabric) together; stop stitching 1/4" from wide (top) end of Blades, **Fig 2**.

2. Sew B Half Blade to one end of fan shape and reversed B Half Blade on other end, **Fig 3**; stop stitching 1/4" from wide (top) end of Blades. Press all the seams in the same direction.

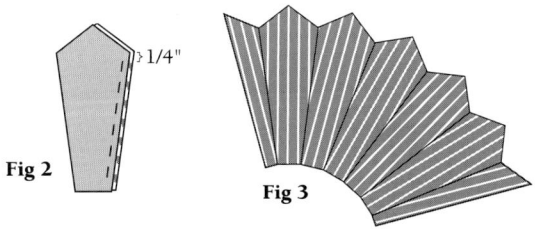

Fig 2

Fig 3

3. Mark center of handle (C Large Quarter Circle) with pin; mark center of fan shape with pin, **Fig 4**. Place fan shape right sides together with handle; match center marks and pin, **Fig 5**. Curve the fan shape to match the curved end of handle; stitch, **Fig 6**.

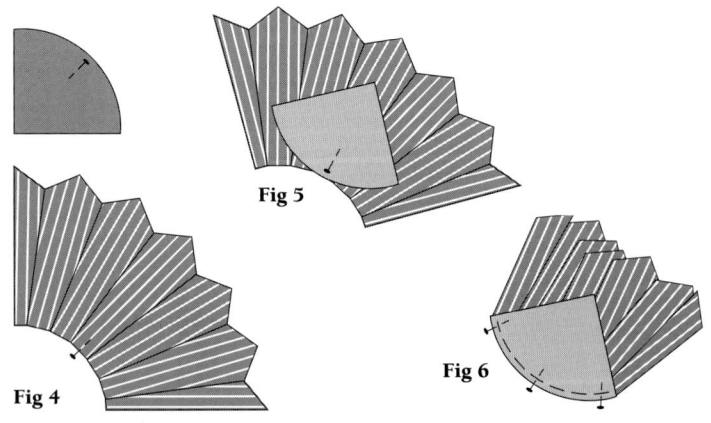

Fig 5

Fig 4

Fig 6

12

4. Press under 1/4" seam allowance on fan blade points. Press point first, then press each side, **Fig 7**.

5. Position fan on background block and blind stitch Blades in place, **Fig 8**.

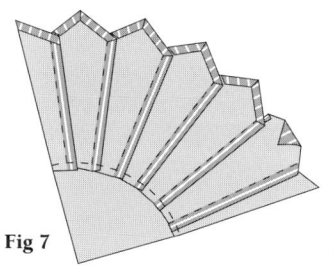
Fig 7
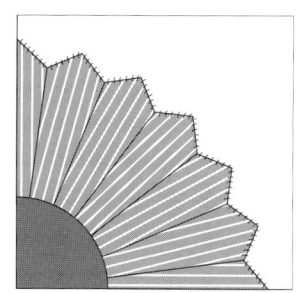
Fig 8

6. Repeat steps 1 through 5 for a total of 30 Fan Blocks.

Finishing

1. For setting squares, mark center of a D Small Quarter Circle and an E Background piece. Place pieces right sides together matching center points; sew. Repeat for a total of 30 setting squares, **Fig 9**.

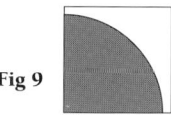
Fig 9

2. Arrange Fan Blocks, lattice strips and setting squares according to layout, noting that top and bottom lattice rows differ from the middle rows. ***Note:*** *Setting squares have the same tie fabric as the fan handle adjacent to it.*

3. Sew blocks and lattice rows together; sew lattice strips and setting squares together. Then sew block rows and lattice rows together.

4. Sew off-white border to sides of quilt; press. Sew off-white border to top and bottom of quilt; press.

5. For outer pieced border, sew two squares of tie fabric together making rectangles, **Fig 10**. Sew pieced rectangle to off-white rectangle, **Fig 11**. Repeat for a total of 66 pieced squares.

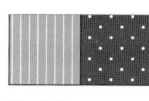
Fig 10
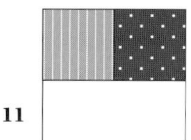
Fig 11

6. For side borders, sew eighteen pieced squares together, alternating directions, **Fig 12**; repeat. Sew to each side of quilt.

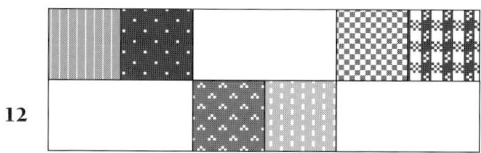
Fig 12

7. For top border, sew 15 pieced squares together, alternating directions; repeat for bottom border.

8. For pieced corner squares, sew 3" off-white square to 3" tie square, **Fig 13**; repeat. Sew to form four patch, **Fig 14**. Repeat for all four corners.

Fig 13
Fig 14

9. Sew four patch to each end of top and bottom borders; sew to quilt.

10. Mark quilting design on quilt top.

11. Layer and baste.

12. Quilt and bind.

13. Sign and date your quilt.

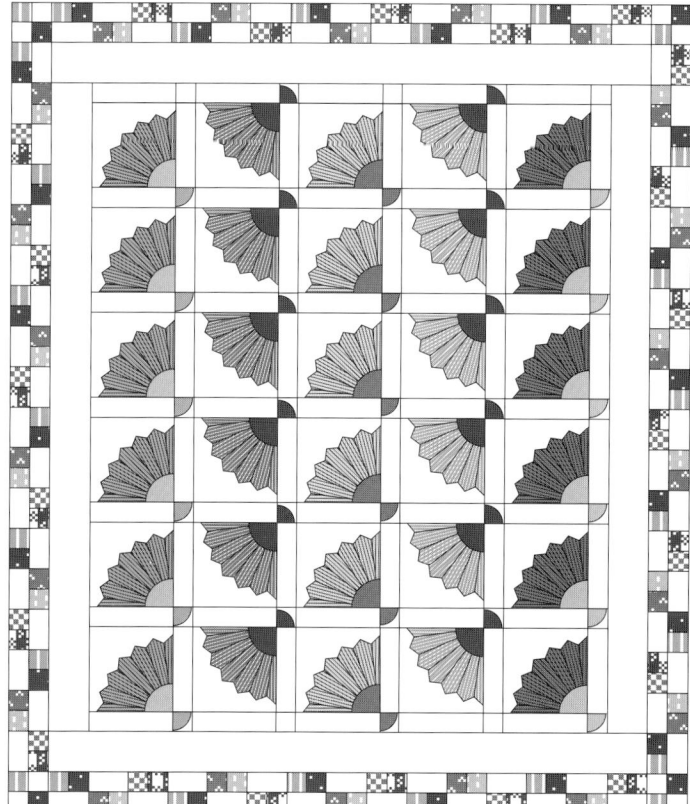
Quilt Layout

13

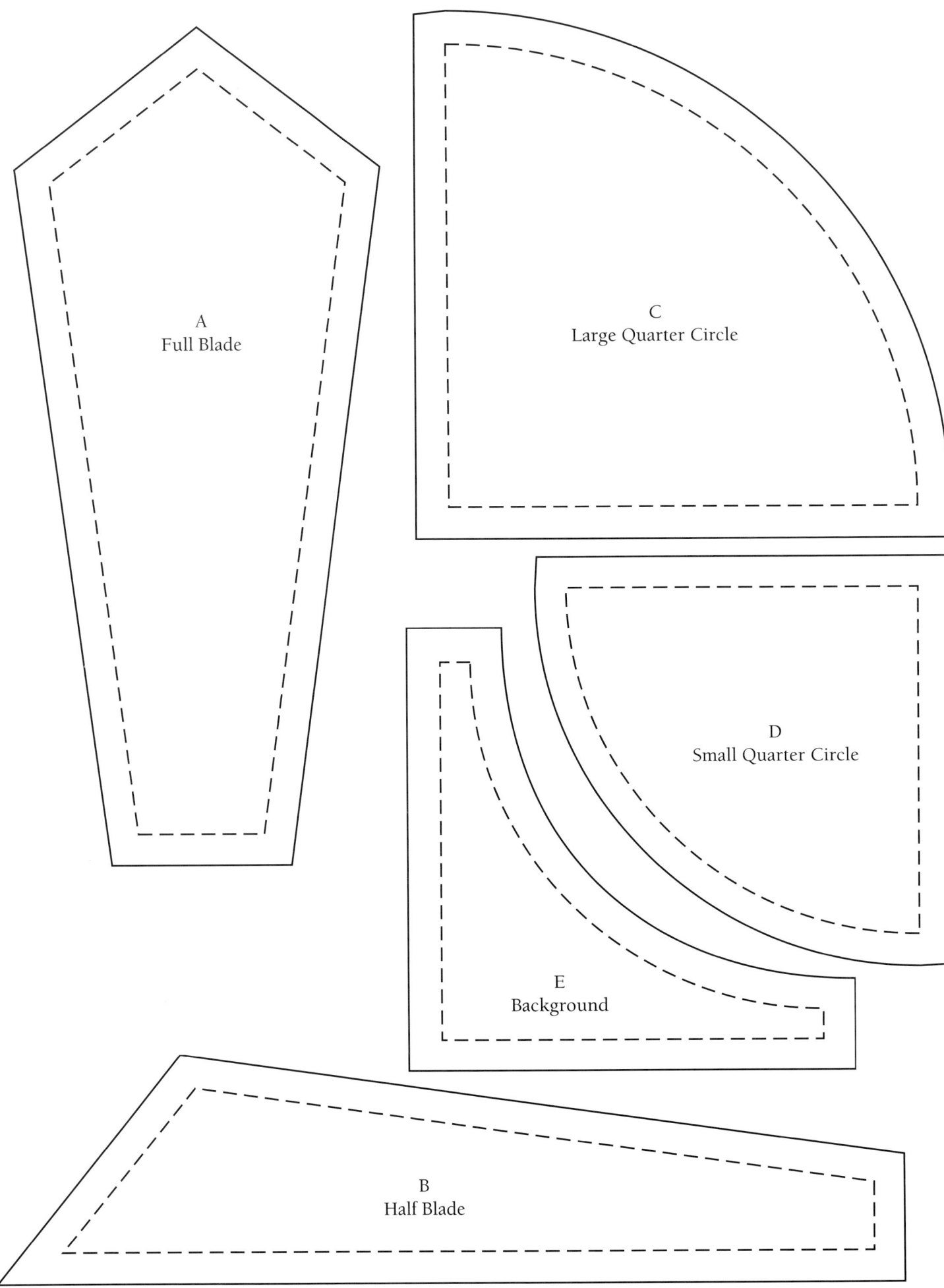

A
Full Blade

C
Large Quarter Circle

D
Small Quarter Circle

E
Background

B
Half Blade

14

Crazy Quilt

Gayle Dodson of Midland, Texas commissioned Linda F. Johnson of Midland, Texas, to make this quilt for "Doc" Dodson using his wool, cotton linen, and polyester ties. The quilt was presented to him on Father's Day, 1990.

Wall Quilt: 42" x 62"

Fabric Requirements:

30 to 50 ties (include some with novelty prints)
1 3/4 yds muslin for foundation
2 1/4 yds black for lining and binding
batting

Cutting List:

Use large sections of novelty patterns. Keep the pointed shape of tie and cut rectangles, squares, and strips. Cut smaller pieces of all over patterns, stripes, and paisley.
42" x 62" rectangle, muslin for foundation

Sewing Instructions:

1. Lay muslin on a flat surface. Position larger pieces of novelty print ties evenly over foundation fabric. Baste in place.

2. Cut random shapes from other patterned ties to fill between larger pieces. Overlap pieces enough for seam allowances, **Fig 1**.

3. Piece together some small shapes into strips that will fill spaces between larger pieces, **Fig 2**.

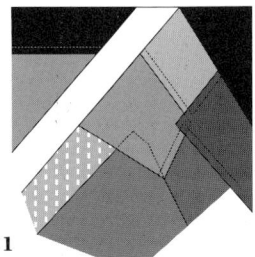

Fig 1   **Fig 2**

4. Continue overlapping pieces of tie fabric until the foundation is covered. Baste in place the pieces that will have other pieces sewn on top. Blind stitch the top pieces in place turning under a 1/4" seam allowance, **Fig 3**.

5. Outline all shapes using different colored threads and a decorative machine embroidery stitch, **Fig 4**.

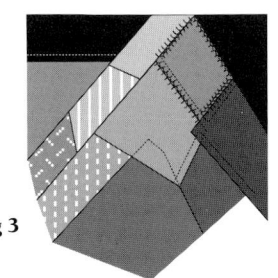
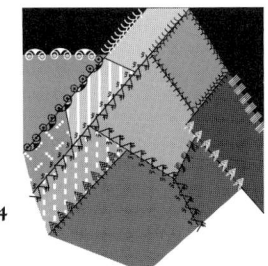

Fig 3   **Fig 4**

Shown in color on page 22

6. Layer quilt top and lining with wrong sides together. Trim lining to match top.

7. Bind.

8. Sign and date your quilt. Gayle Dodson used tags from the ties used in the quilt as part of her quilt label.

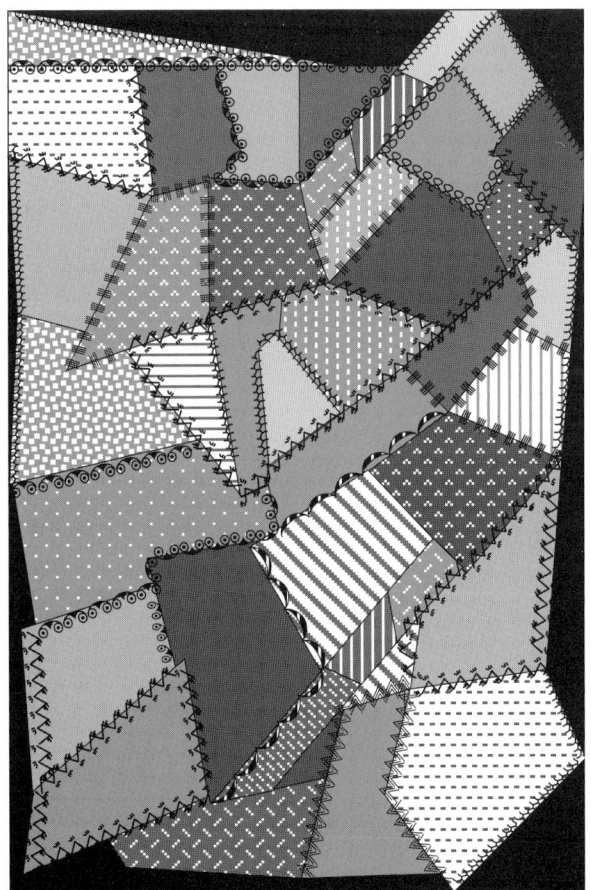

Quilt Layout

Tumbling Blocks

Suzanne Cline McGann of Lubbock, Texas stitched this wall quilt as a gift for her son, Jim.

Wall Quilt: 37 1/2" x 36"

Fabric Requirements:
22 light-colored ties
22 medium-colored ties
22 dark-colored ties
2 1/2 yds black for background, lining and tabs

Pattern Pieces:
A Diamond
B Half Diamond
C Wedge

Cutting List:
Note: Trace pattern pieces onto template plastic; trace templates onto wrong side of fabric, leaving at least 1/2" in between each piece. Cut out pieces 1/4" beyond traced line.
22 A Diamonds, light-colored ties*
22 A Diamonds, medium-colored ties*
22 A Diamonds, dark-colored ties*
six C Wedges, black
ten B Half Diamonds, black
two 3" x 31" border strips, black
two 3" x 38" border strips, black
nine 3" x 3" squares, black (hanging tabs)
*Consider sometimes using the wrong side of the tie fabrics in order to create the contrast needed for this pattern.

Sewing Instructions:
1. Sew a light-colored A Diamond and a medium-colored A Diamond along one edge following traced line, **Fig 1**.

2. Sew dark-colored A Diamond between light-colored and medium-colored A Diamonds along drawn line; stitch from inside corner toward outer edge, **Fig 2**.

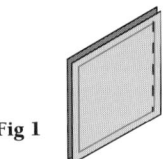
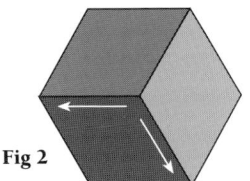

3. Repeat steps 1 and 2 for a total of 22 blocks keeping light, medium and dark A Diamonds in same position for every block.

4. Referring to Quilt Layout, arrange blocks starting with four in the first row, five in the next row, and so on for a total of five rows. Sew blocks together in rows, then sew rows together.

Shown in color on page 24

5. Sew short, straight edge of C Wedges to blocks on each side of quilt, **Fig 3**. Sew diagonal edges together starting from inside corner going toward outside edge, **Fig 4**.

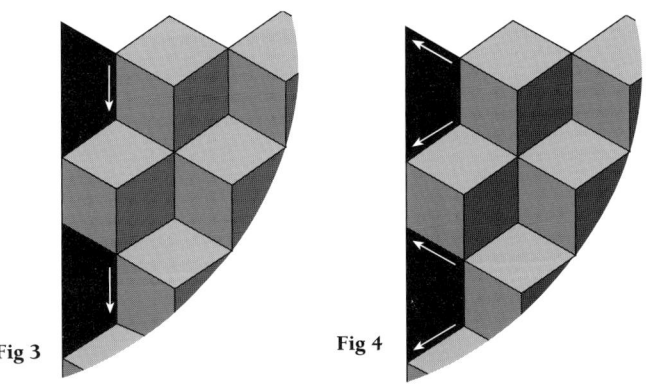

6. Sew B Half Diamonds to blocks along top and bottom edges of quilt top. Stitch from inside corner toward outside edge, **Fig 5**.

7. Sew C Wedges to B Half Diamonds at corners in same manner, **Fig 6**.

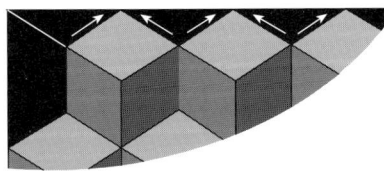
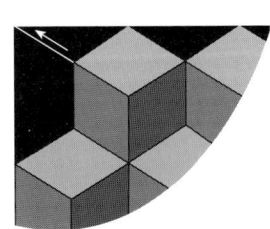

8. Add borders to sides first, then top and bottom.

9. For tabs, fold 3" squares in half with right sides together; stitch along long edge with a 1/4" seam allowance, **Fig 7**. Turn right side out; position seam in middle and press, **Fig 8**. Repeat for a total of 9 tabs.

10. Fold tabs in half crosswise; pin at equal intervals across top of quilt, **Fig 9**.

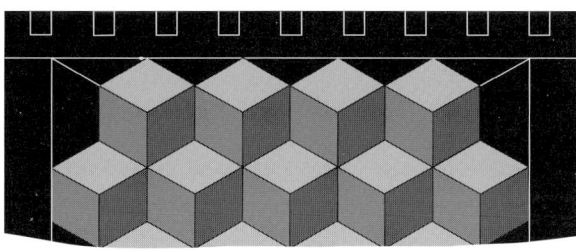

Fig 9

11. Place lining and quilt top with right sides together. **Note:** *If using batting, place under lining.* Sew along edge of quilt using a 1/4" seam allowance; leave an opening about 6" long in center of one side.

12. Turn quilt right side out; press. Blind stitch opening closed.

13. Sign and date your quilt.

14. Mount on drapery rod through tabs.

Quilt Layout

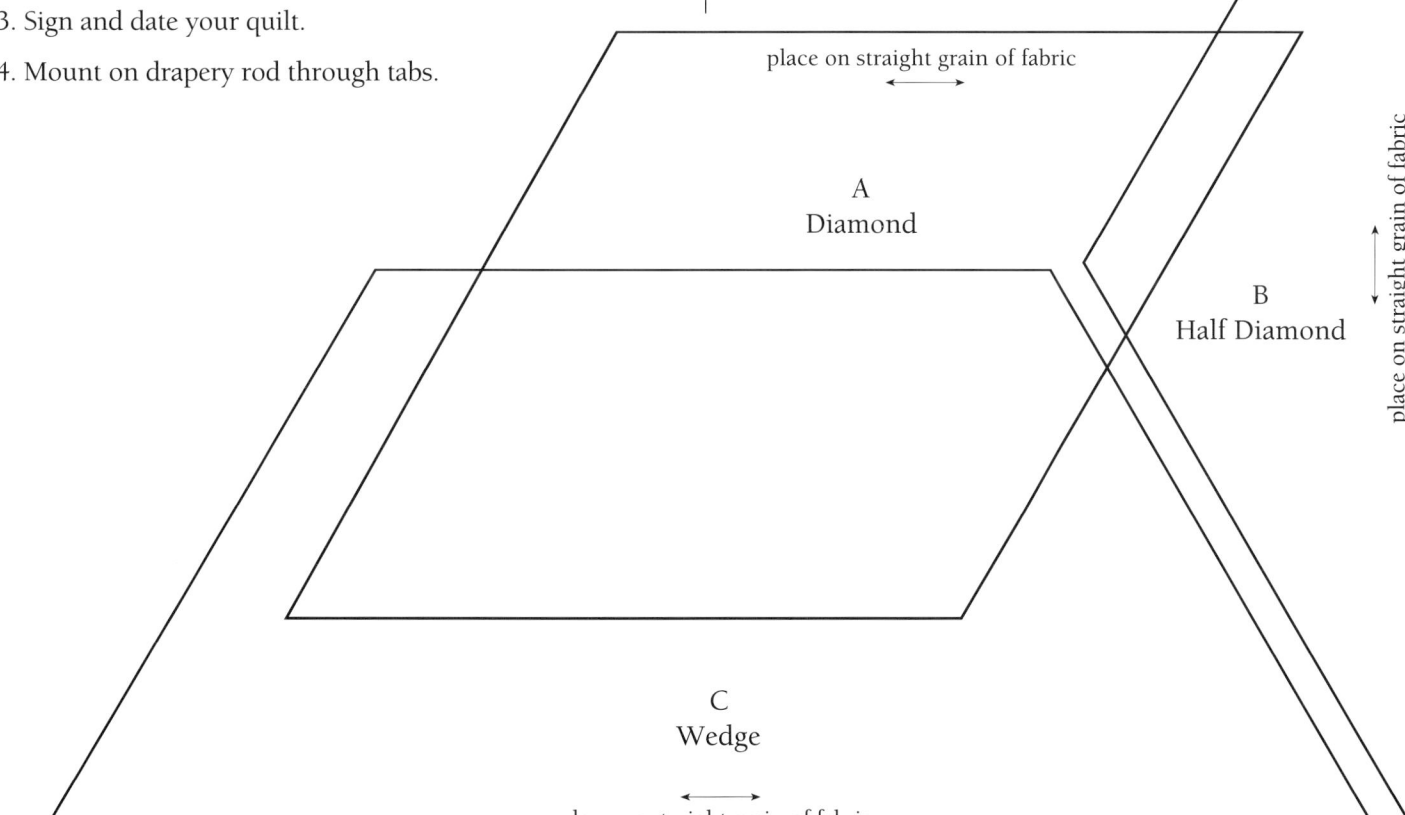

place on straight grain of fabric

A
Diamond

B
Half Diamond

place on straight grain of fabric

C
Wedge

place on straight grain of fabric

17

Grandpa Glenn's Necktie Quilt

Nancy Carelene Simmons Richburg lives in Plainview, Texas and loves to make quilts. She made this quilt completely by machine using the 90 ties left when her Grandpa Glenn died in 1990 at age 93.

Double Size Quilt: 76" x 100"

Fabric Requirements:

112 assorted ties (you will need to get at least three A Blades from each tie)

15 yds black solid for background, border, and lining

2 3/4 yds red solid for first border

batting

Additional Supplies:

tear away stabilizer (for machine embroidery)

thread, black, white, and bold, bright colors

erasable white fabric pencil

Note: Decorative seams are stitched using a sewing machine that offers a variety of stitches.

Pattern Pieces:

A Blade

B Quarter Circle

Cutting List:

336 A Blades, assorted ties

48 - 13" x 13" squares, black (allows for shrinkage from embroidery)

48 B Quarter Circles, black

two 1 1/4" x 96 1/2", red (first border)

two 1 1/4" x 74", red (first border)

eight 3" squares, red (second border)

four 3" x 28", black (second border)

two 3" x 38", black (second border)

two 3" x 76 1/2", black (second border)

Sewing Instructions:

Making the Blocks

1. Fold A Blade in half lengthwise with right sides together, **Fig 1**.

2. Sew across wide end, **Fig 2**; clip corner at fold, **Fig 3**.

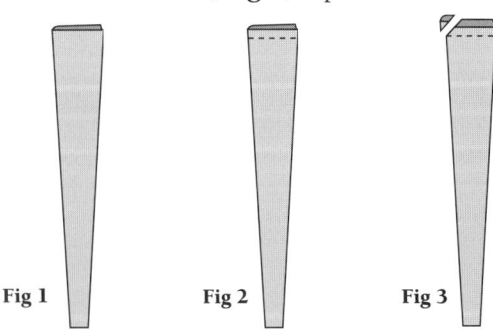

Fig 1   Fig 2   Fig 3

Shown in color on back cover

3. Turn Blade right side out, forming a point, **Fig 4**; press.

4. Repeat steps 1 to 3 for all 336 blades.

5. Sew seven Blades together to form a fan, **Fig 5**. Mix colors and prints to keep variety in the blocks. Press seams open to distribute bulk.

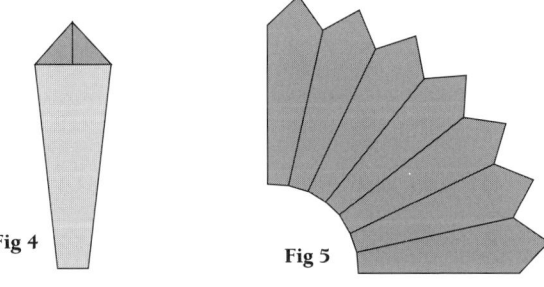

Fig 4   Fig 5

6. Mark a diagonal line across 13" background square using an erasable white fabric pencil.

7. Position fan on the background square with the point from the center Blade on the diagonal line; the closest tip of the fan should be about 3/4" from the edge of the block, **Fig 6**.

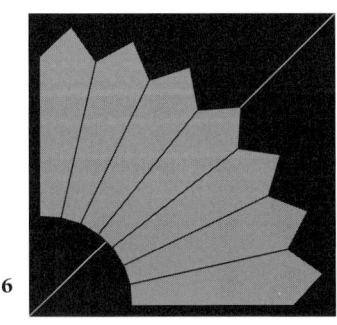

Fig 6

8. Pin each seam of the fan to the background in at least three places, **Fig 7**. Sew a basting stitch along each seam line beginning with the center seam and working out. If machine basting, use a walking foot and invisible thread.

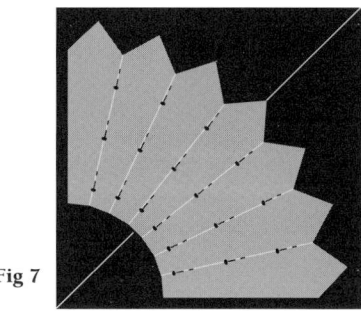

Fig 7

9. Repeat steps 5 to 8 for 48 blocks.

10. Decorate each seam using different color threads and different decorative embroidery stitches, **Fig 8**. *Hint: Use the same color thread on several different blocks before changing thread color.*

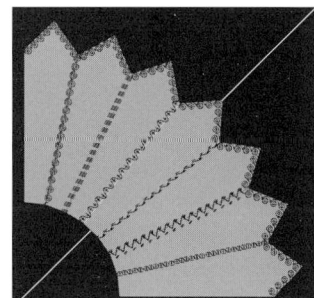

Fig 8

11. When all seams have been stitched, outline the fan with another stitch and color. *Hint: Choose a stitch that will turn the corners and points easily.*

12. *Optional:* For decorative stitching on B Quarter Circles, it is best to do the stitching before cutting them out of the fabric. Draw 48 B Quarter Circles on the background fabric leaving room between each for seam allowances. *Hint: Use tear-away stabilizer under the background fabric to help keep the work smooth. Then, place area to be stitched in an embroidery hoop to keep work taut. Stitch in Quarter Circles as desired.*

13. Cut out the 48 (decorated) Quarter Circles, allowing 1/4" seam allowances. Stay stitch on the seam line of the curved edge of each quarter circle, **Fig 9**. Clip almost to the stitching, **Fig 10;** press under the seam allowance.

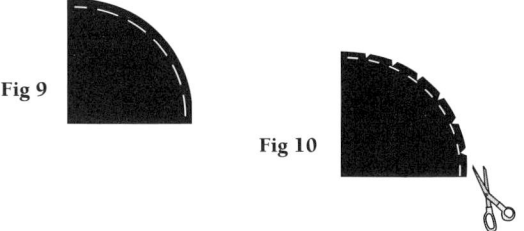

Fig 9

Fig 10

14. Pin the Quarter Circles in place on the blocks, overlapping ends of fan, **Fig 11**. Use another decorative stitch and thread color to attach Quarter Circle along curved edge to block.

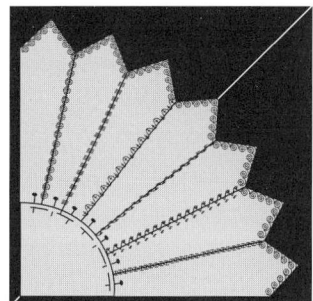

Fig 11

15. Trim each block to measure 12 1/2" x 12 1/2". Then cut background fabric away under the Quarter Circle.

Quilt Layout

Finishing

1. Arrange blocks according to the Quilt Layout.

2. Sew each row of blocks together; press. Use a contrasting thread and decorative stitch to decorate each seam.

3. Join rows in pairs; press. Decorate the seam. Join two pairs of rows; press. Decorate the seam. Join the two four-row sections; press. Decorate the final seam.

4. Sew red border to sides of quilt first, then to top and bottom; press. Stitch along seam with decorative stitch using white or contrasting thread.

5. Decorate the eight 3" red squares with machine embroidery being sure to stitch 1/4" from raw edges.

6. For side borders, sew a decorated square to each end of 3" x 38" black strip; sew 3" x 28" black strip to sides of each red square, **Fig 12**. Repeat for one more strip. Stitch to each side of quilt top.

Fig 12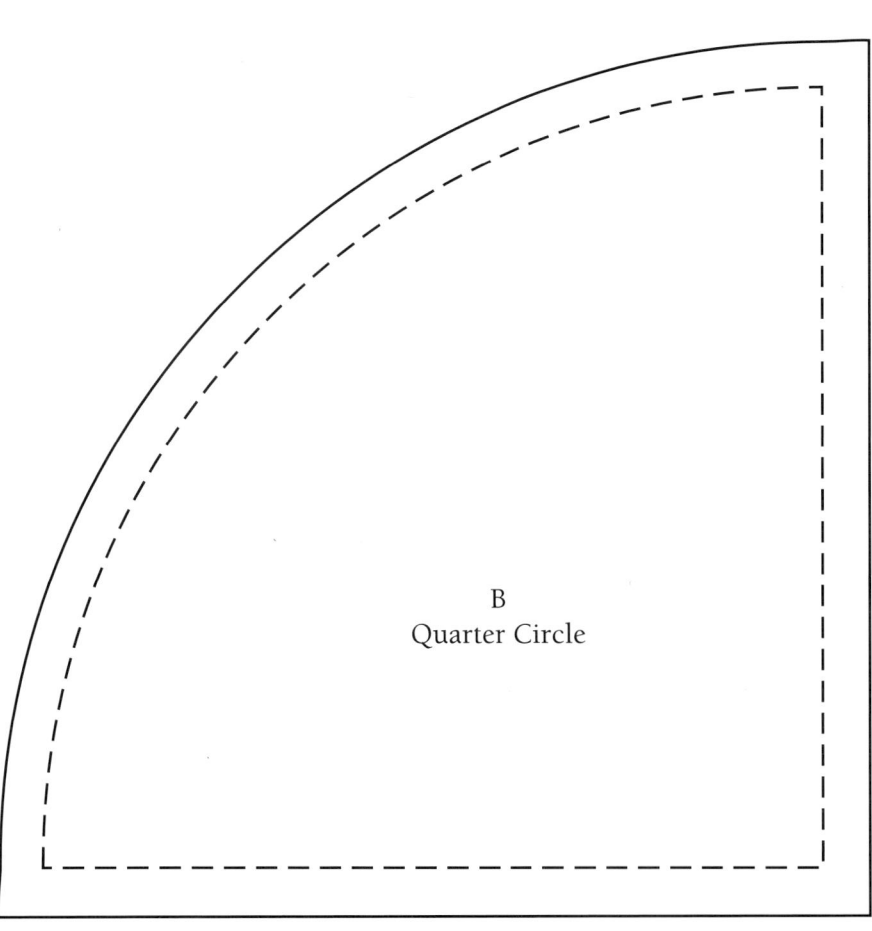

7. For top and bottom border, sew red square at each end of 3" x 76 1/2" black strip; repeat. Sew borders to top and bottom of quilt top.

8. Layer quilt top, batting and lining. Baste to keep layers together.

9. Use sewing machine or hand tack invisibly about every 8" over entire quilt.

10. Trim batting even with edge of quilt top. Trim lining 1" larger than quilt top.

11. Fold lining over edge of quilt toward top, turning under a 1/4" seam allowance. Using black thread, sew along folded edge with decorative machine stitch to attach lining to quilt top.

12. Sign and date your quilt.

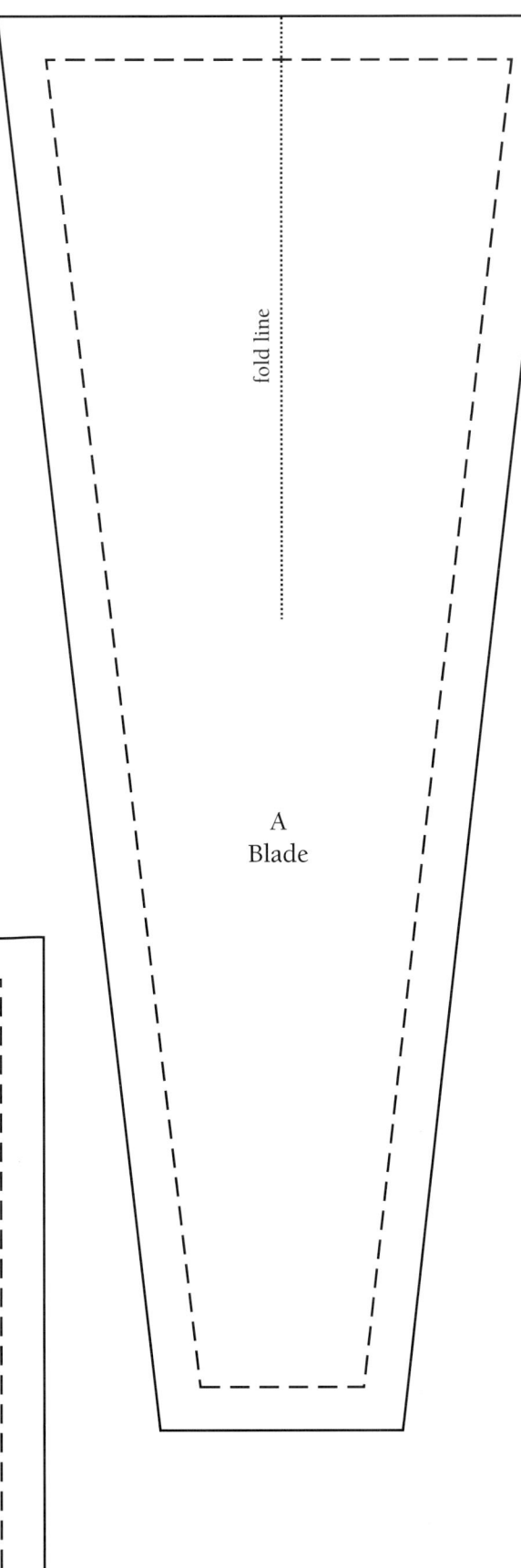

fold line

A
Blade

B
Quarter Circle

Sunburst, *page 26*

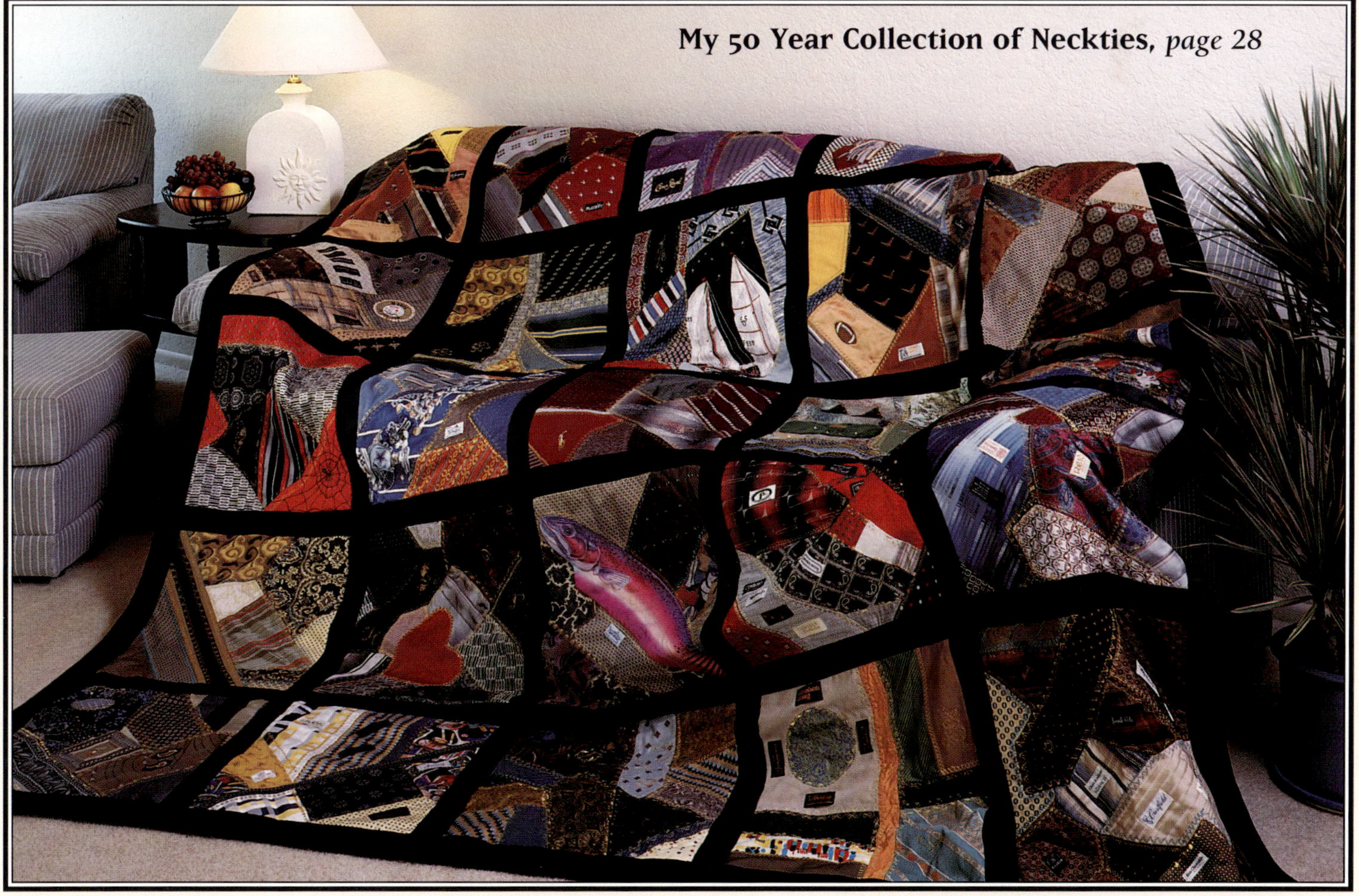

My 50 Year Collection of Neckties, *page 28*

Crazy Quilt, *page 15*

Fan Fantasy, *page 12*

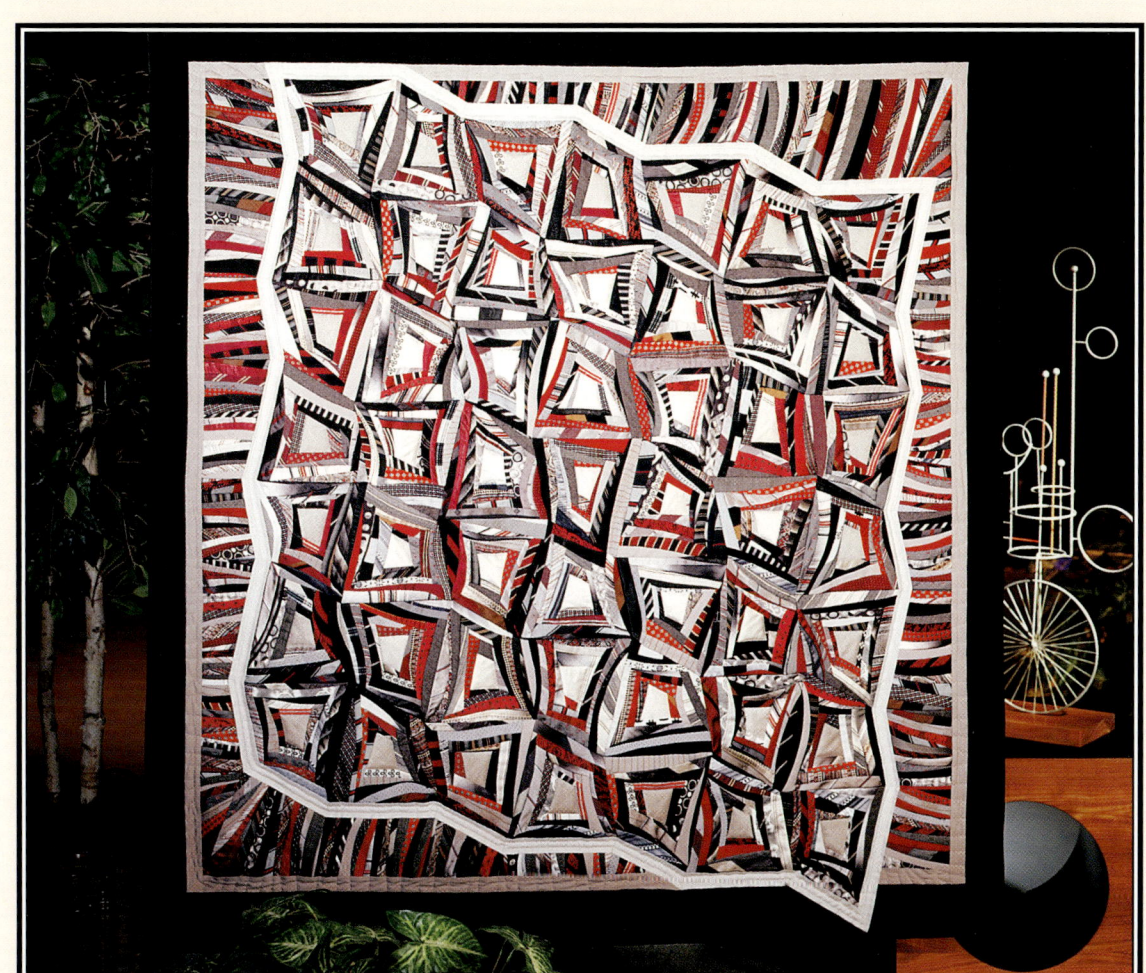

Tessellating Ties, *page 41*

Retired Ties, *page 8*

Joel's Star, *page 36*

Charming Bricks, *page 25*

Tumbling Blocks, *page 16*

Charming Bricks

There are no pattern repeats in this easy-to-stitch quilt made by Sharon Newman in 1995.

Double Size Quilt: 69" x 85"

Fabric Requirements:

246 assorted ties
3 yds black solid for lattice and binding
4 yds fabric for lining

Cutting List:

230 - 3 1/2" x 5 1/2" rectangles, assorted ties
16 - 3 1/2" x 2 1/2" rectangles, assorted ties
18 - 1 1/2" x 84" strips, black solid for long lattice
two 1 1/2" x 70" strips, black solid for medium lattice
229 - 1 1/2" x 3 1/2" strips, black solid for short lattice

Sewing Instructions:

1. Referring to Quilt Layout, arrange tie rectangles in 17 vertical rows. Every other row will begin and end with a 2 1/2" x 3 1/2" rectangle. Ties may be arranged at random or grouped by color according to the collection.

2. For Row 1, sew thirteen 1 1/2" x 3 1/2" black lattice strips alternately with fourteen 3 1/2" x 5 1/2" rectangles; begin and end with a rectangle. Repeat for a total of nine rows. Press seam allowances toward the lattice.

3. For Row 2, sew fourteen 1 1/2" x 3 1/2" lattice strips alternately with thirteen 3 1/2" x 5 1/2" rectangles; begin and end with a lattice strip. Sew a 2 1/2" x 3 1/2" rectangle to each end. Repeat for a total of eight rows.

4. Mark one edge of each 1 1/2" x 84" long lattice strip to correspond with Row 1: 1/4" for seam allowance, then 5" for rectangle, 1" for lattice, 5", 1", and so on, ending with a final 1/4" seam, **Fig 1**. Mark the other edge of all but two long lattice strips to correspond with Row 2: start with 1/4" seam allowance, then 2", 1", 5" 1" 5" and so on, ending with 2" and 1/4", **Fig 2**.

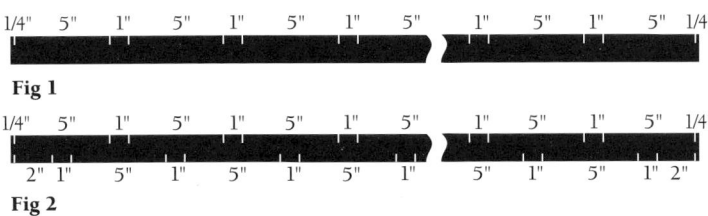

Fig 1

Fig 2

5. Pin rows to lattice strips (with both sides marked) matching marks with seams; sew. Press all seams toward lattice. Pin lattice strips with one edge marked to sides; sew. Press seams toward lattice.

Shown in color on page 24

6. Mark one edge of each 1 1/2" x 70" medium lattice strip to correspond with top and bottom seams: 1/4" for seam, then 3" for each rectangle and 1" for each lattice, ending with a 1/4" seam, **Fig 3**.

Fig 3

7. Pin top and bottom lattice matching marks with seams; sew. Press all seams toward lattice.

8. Mark quilting design.

9. Layer and baste.

10. Quilt and bind.

11. Sign and date your quilt.

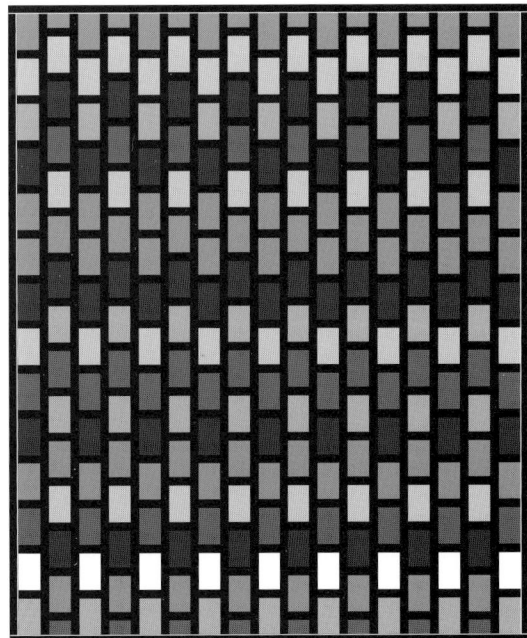

Quilt Layout

25

Sunburst

Margie Rhoads of Crosbyton, Texas made this quilt in 1984, as a surprise for her husband. He liked the quilt but was unhappy that she had used his favorite red tie.

King Size Quilt: 97" x 97"

Fabric Requirements:

32 assorted ties
18 yds cream for background and lining
1 1/2 yds print for center and binding
batting

Pattern Piece:

A Quarter Circle

Cutting List:

one 15" diameter circle (using Quarter Circle pattern),
  print
2 1/2"-wide strips totaling 400", print for binding
two 42" (full width) x 100" lengths, cream fabric
  for background and lining
four 30" x 100" lengths, cream fabric for background
  and lining

Sewing Instructions:

1. Remove interlining and lining from all 32 ties; press back into original tie shape.

2. Cut 16 ties about 30 1/2" long, and 16 ties about 35 1/2" long measuring from point of wider end.

3. Sew a 30" wide length of cream fabric on each side of a full width piece, **Fig 1**. Repeat for lining.

Fig 1

4. Fold background into halves, then fourths; mark center, **Fig 2**.

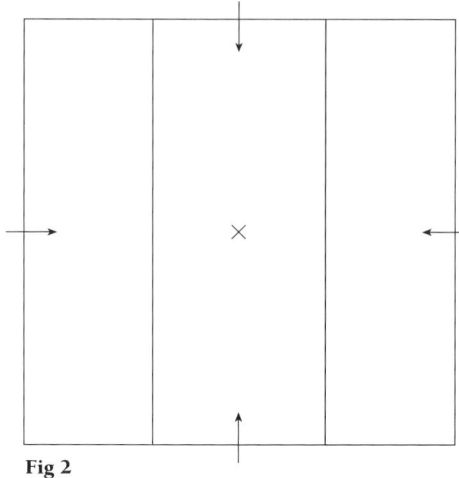

Fig 2

5. Clip curved edge of print Circle making 1/4" clips; press under 1/4" seam allowance around print circle. Place circle at center of quilt top, **Fig 3**; pin in place. Position ties around center alternating the short and long lengths, **Fig 4**; insert cut edge of ties 1/2" under print circle.

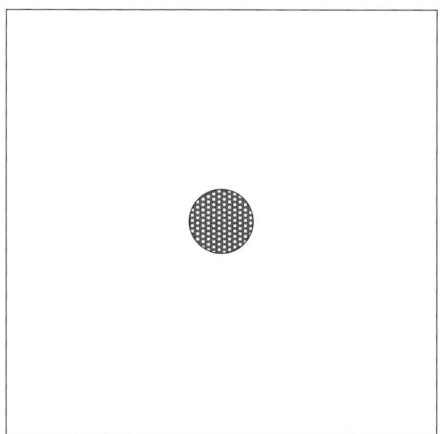

Fig 3

Fig 4

6. Machine zigzag ties in place with matching thread.

7. After all ties have been stitched in place, machine zigzag print circle covering raw edges of ties.

8. Mark lines for quilting design.

9. Layer and baste.

10. Quilt and bind.

11. Sign and date your quilt.

A
Quarter Circle

Note: *Trace 4 times onto large piece of tracing paper, rotating a quarter turn each time to make 15" diameter circle.*

My 50 Year Collection of Neckties, 1940-1990

Donna Phillips of Lubbock, Texas made this king-size quilt as a gift for her husband who has worn all the ties in their large collection. Donna has been quilting for several years and enjoys making a variety of patterns.

King Size Quilt: 92" X 110"

Fabric Requirements:

75 to 100 assorted ties
10 yds 60"-wide black for lattice, lining, binding
7 1/2 yds muslin for foundation squares
batting

Additional Supplies:

gold metallic thread
black perle cotton thread, size 5

Cutting List:

30 - 17 1/2" squares, muslin (allows for shrinkage
   from embroidery)
24 - 2 1/2" x 16 1/2" lattice strips, black
seven 2 1/2" x 88 1/2" lattice strips, black
two 2 1/2" x 110 1/2" lattice strips, black
2 1/2"-wide binding strips totalling 410", black
random-shaped pieces, assorted ties

Sewing Instructions:

1. Choose a "theme" tie for the center piece of each block. Center a large piece of the theme tie diagonally on the 17 1/2" muslin square foundation.

2. Place a piece from a coordinating tie right sides together with the theme tie; sew 1/4" from raw edges through foundation, **Fig 1**. Fold piece over seam allowance, press and trim even with first piece, **Fig 2**.

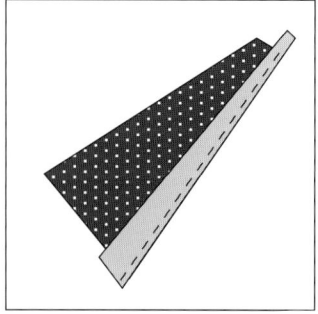

Fig 1

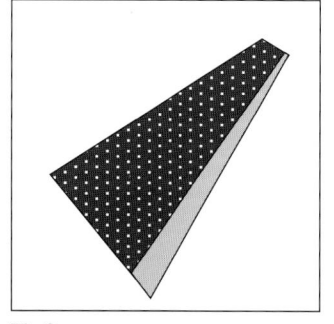

Fig 2

Shown in color on page 21

3. Working from the center of the square to the outside edge, continue adding tie pieces until entire foundation is covered, **Fig 3**.

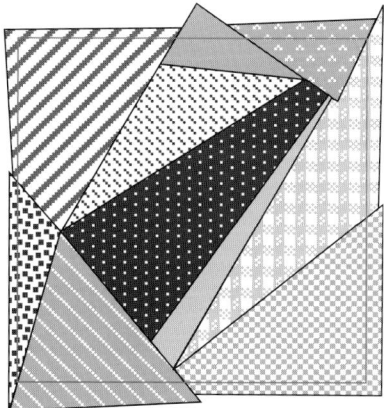

Fig 3

If you get caught in a corner, blind stitch the next piece in place by hand turning under a 1/4" seam, **Fig 4**.

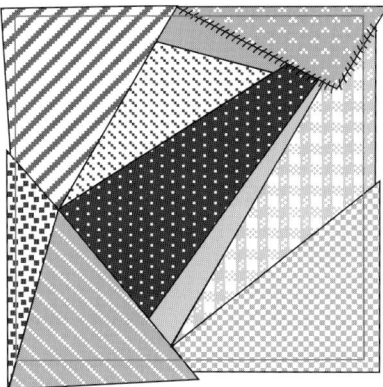

Fig 4

4. When all the foundations have been covered with tie pieces, add machine embroidery stitches and embellishments on each block. The designer used labels from the ties to embellish some of the blocks.

5. Trim all blocks to 16 1/2" x 16 1/2".

6. Referring to Quilt Layout, arrange blocks five across and six down.

7. Sew 2 1/2" x 16 1/2" black lattice strips between blocks in each row.

8. Join rows with 2 1/2" x 88 1/2" black lattice strips between each row and at top and bottom.

9. Sew 2 1/2" x 110 1/2" black strips to each side of quilt top.

10. Layer and baste.

11. Tack quilt with perle cotton thread at intersections of lattice, and at center of each block edge.

12. Trim batting and lining to match quilt top.

13. Bind.

14. Sign and date your quilt.

Quilt Layout

Sampler

Sharon Newman of Lubbock, Texas, made this quilt using a small collection of neckties. The blocks depict the interests of the owner of the ties.

Wall Quilt: 22 1/2" x 22 1/2"

Fabric Requirements:

20 to 30 ties in coordinating colors of light to
    dark brown and light to dark blue
scrap, red print tie
scrap, yellow print tie
2/3 yd fabric for backing
one fat quarter (18" x 22") each, dk brown and lt brown for
    binding
batting

Additional Supplies:

perle cotton, size 5 for tying

Pattern Pieces:

A Square
B Triangle
C Small Trapezoid
D Long Trapezoid and reversed
E Medium Trapezoid
F Large Trapezoid and reversed
G Triangle
H Triangle
I Trapezoid and reversed
J Background Triangle and reversed
K Roof
L Roof Triangle
M Boat
N Triangle
O Square
P Triangle

Cutting List:

Economy Block
two A Squares, dk brown tie
two A Squares, med blue tie
eight B Triangles, lt blue tie
eight B Triangles, med brown tie

Crayon Box Block
one 2 1/2" square, dk brown tie
six 1 1/2" x 2 1/2" strips, dk brown tie
four 1 1/2" x 3 1/2" strips, med blue tie
two 1 1/2" x 4 1/2" strips, med brown tie

Lone Eagle Block
two 3/4" x 2 3/4" strips, med blue tie
one D Long Trapezoid and one reversed, med blue tie

Shown in color on back cover

one F Large Trapezoid and one reversed , med blue tie
two 1 1/2" x 2 3/4" strips, med blue
one 3/4" x 2" strip, dk brown
one C Small Trapezoid, dk brown
one 2" x 6 1/2" strip, med brown tie
one E Medium Trapezoid, dk brown tie
one 1 1/2" x 2" strip, dk brown tie

Picket Fences Block
two H Small Triangles, lt blue tie
two H Small Triangles, med blue tie
two G Large Triangles, lt brown tie
two G Large Triangles, dk brown tie
two I Trapezoids and two reversed, dk brown tie

His House Block
one K Roof, dk brown tie
one L Roof Triangle, med brown tie
one 1 1/2" square, red tie (chimney)
one 1 1/2" square, lt blue tie (sky)
one 1 1/2" x 4 1/2" strip, lt blue tie (sky)
one J Background Triangle and one reversed,
    lt blue tie (sky)
one 1 1/4" x 4 1/2" strips, lt brown tie
one 1 1/4" x 2 1/2" strip, lt brown tie
two 1" x 2 3/4" strips, lt brown tie (door sides)
one 1 1/2" x 2 3/4" strip, dk brown tie (door)
two 1 1/4" x 1 3/4" strip, lt brown tie (window sides)
one 1" x 1 3/4" strip, lt brown tie (window side)
two 1 1/2" x 1 3/4" rectangles, yellow tie (windows)
one 1 1/2" x 4 1/2" strip, lt brown tie (bottom of windows)

Pinwheels Block
eight B Small Triangles, lt brown tie
eight B Small Triangles, dk brown tie
two 3 1/2" squares, brown/blue tie

The Ship Block

four B Triangles, med blue tie
six B Triangles, lt blue tie
two 2" x 3 1/2" rectangles, lt blue tie
one M Boat, dk brown tie
one 2" x 6 1/2" strip, dk blue tie

Card Trick Block

one O Square, dk brown tie
four P Small Triangles, med blue print tie
four N Medium Triangles, med blue print tie
four N Medium Triangles, dk brown tie
four H Large Triangles, med blue/gray tie
four H Large Triangles, med blue print tie
four H Large Triangles, med brown tie

Four Patch Block

four 2" squares, brown solid tie
four 2" squares, dk blue tie
two P Triangles, dk brown tie
two P Triangles, blue stripe tie

Lattice Strips

twelve 1 1/2" x 6 1/2" strips, lt brown tie
twelve 1 1/2" x 6 1/2" strips, dk brown tie
sixteen 1 1/2" x 1 1/2" squares, dk blue tie

Binding

two 1 1/2" x 16" bias strips, lt brown tie
two 1 1/2" x 30" bias strips, dark brown tie

Sewing Instructions:

Hints: Keep fabric pieces for each block together to prevent an error while sewing. Press after each step.

Economy Block

1. Following **Fig 1**, sew two lt blue B Triangles to opposite sides of dk brown A Square; sew lt blue B Triangles to remaining two sides. Repeat step 1 for another square.

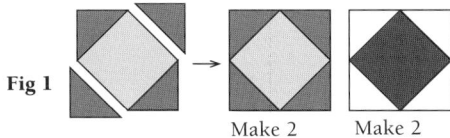

Fig 1   Make 2   Make 2

2. Repeat step 1 sewing a med brown B Triangles to med blue A Square. Repeat for another square.

3. Sew pieced squares in pairs; repeat. Sew pairs together to complete Economy Block, **Fig 2**; press.

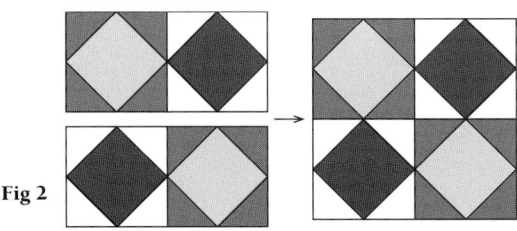

Fig 2   Economy Block

Crayon Box Block

Refer to **Fig 3** for the following steps:

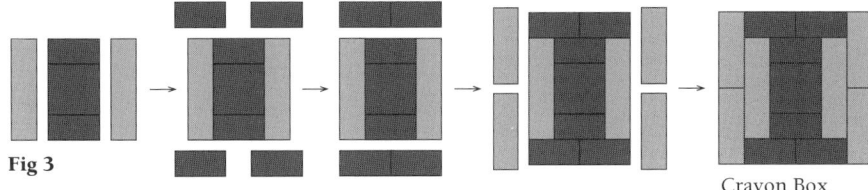

Fig 3   Crayon Box

1. Sew 1 1/2" x 2 1/2" dk brown strip to top and bottom of 2 1/2" square. Sew a 1 1/2" x 4 1/2" med brown strip to each side.

2. Sew two 1 1/2" x 2 1/2" dk brown strips together; repeat. Sew to top and bottom; press.

3. Sew two 1 1/2" x 3 1/2" med blue strips together; repeat. Sew to sides to complete Crayon Box Block.

Lone Eagle Block

Follow **Fig 4** for the following steps:

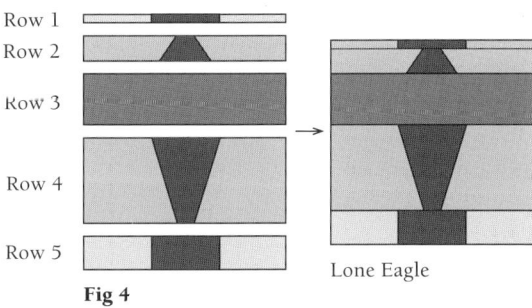

Row 1
Row 2
Row 3
Row 4
Row 5
Fig 4   Lone Eagle

1. For row 1, sew 3/4" x 2 3/4" med blue strips to each end of 3/4" x 2" dk brown strip.

2. For row 2, sew med blue D Trapezoid and reversed D Trapezoid to dk brown C Trapezoid .

3. For row 4, sew med blue F Trapezoid and reversed F Trapezoid to dk brown E Trapezoid.

4. For row 5, sew med blue 1 1/2" x 2 3/4" strip to opposite ends of dk brown 1 1/2" x 2" strip.

5. Sew rows 1 and 2 together; sew to 2" x 6 1/2" med brown strip (row 3).

6. Sew rows 4 and 5 together; then sew to upper half to complete Lone Eagle Block.

Picket Fences Block

1. Sew dk brown G Triangle to lt brown G Triangle to make a large pieced square, **Fig 5**; repeat.

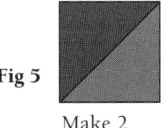

Fig 5   Make 2

2. Sew a lt blue H Triangle to a med blue H Triangle to make small pieced square; repeat.

3. Sew dk brown I Trapezoid to med blue side of small pieced square; stop sewing 1/4" from diagonal edge of Trapezoid, **Fig 6**. Repeat with dk brown reversed I Trapezoid on adjacent edge of pieced square.

4. Join diagonal seam from edge of square to outer edge of strip, **Fig 7**; press.

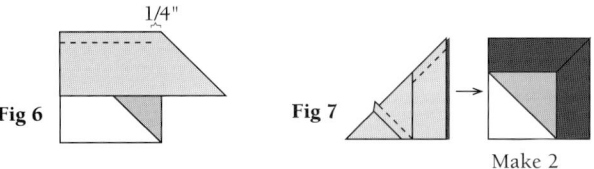

Fig 6   Fig 7

Make 2

5. Repeat steps 2 to 5 for another block.

6. Join the four pieced units to complete Picket Fences Block, **Fig 8**; press.

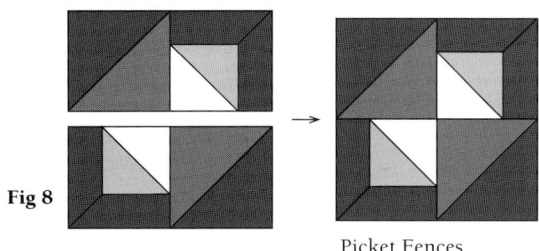

Fig 8

Picket Fences

His House Block

Refer to **Fig 9** for the following steps:

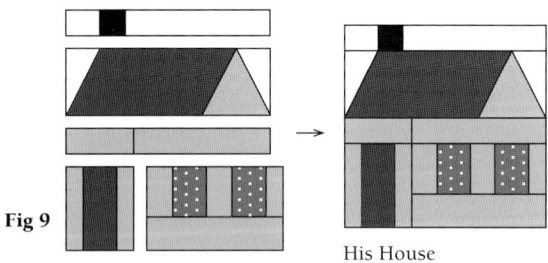

Fig 9

His House

1. For row 1, sew lt blue 1 1/2" square, 1 1/2" red square, and 1 1/2" x 4 1/2" lt blue strip,.

2. For row 2, sew lt blue J Background Triangle, dk brown K Roof, med brown L Roof Triangle and lt blue reversed J Background Triangle.

3. Join rows 1 and 2.

4. For row 3, sew med brown 1 1/4" x 2 1/2" strip to med brown 1 1/4" x 4 1/2" strip.

5. For window section, sew med brown 1 1/4" x 1 3/4" strip, yellow 1 1/2" x 1 3/4" rectangle, med brown 1 1/4" x 1 3/4" strip, yellow 1 1/2" x 1 3/4" rectangle and med brown 1" x 1 3/4" strip. Sew med brown 1 1/2" x 4 1/2" strip to bottom edge.

6. For door section, sew a med brown 1" x 2 3/4" strip to opposite sides of dk brown 1 1/2" x 2 3/4" strip.

7. Join the door section to the window section; then sew row 3 to top edge. Sew house section to roof section to complete His House Block.

Pinwheels Block

1. Sew a dk brown B Triangle to a lt brown B Triangle to make pieced square, **Fig 10**. Make 8.

2. Sew two pieced squares together; repeat. Sew pairs of squares together to make a pinwheel, **Fig 11**.

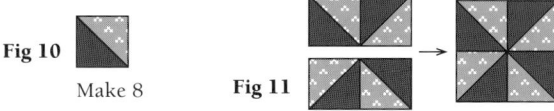

Fig 10

Make 8   Fig 11

3. Sew pinwheel to 3 1/2" square; repeat. Then, sew rows together to complete Pinwheels Block, **Fig 12**.

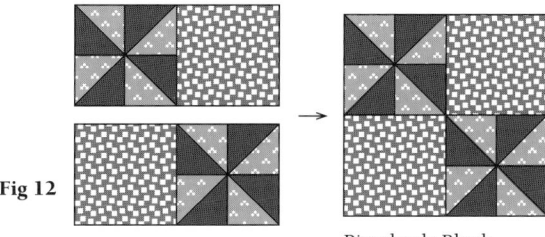

Fig 12

Pinwheels Block

The Ship Block

1. Sew a lt blue B Triangle and a med blue B Triangle together, **Fig 13**. Make 4.

2. Referring to **Fig 14**, stitch two rows with two squares each; join rows for sails. Sew lt blue 2" x 3 1/2" rectangle on each side of sails.

Fig 13

Make 4

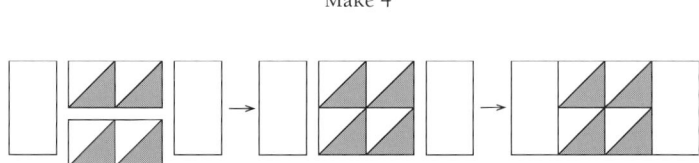

Fig 14

3. Sew a lt blue B Triangle to each end of M Boat; sew dk blue 2" x 6 1/2" strip to Boat, **Fig 15**.

4. Sew sail section to boat section to complete The Ship Block, **Fig 16**.

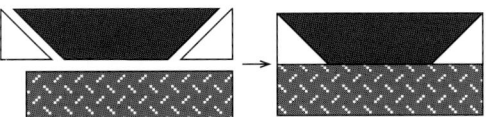

Fig 15

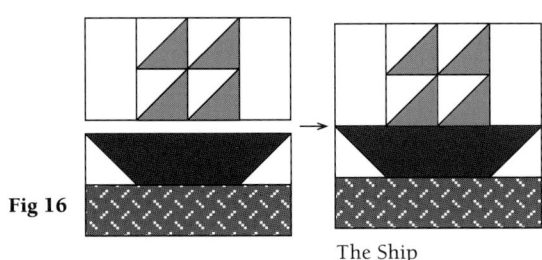

Fig 16

The Ship

Card Trick Block

1. Sew a med brown H Triangle to a med blue H Triangle to make a square, **Fig 17**. Make 4.

2. Sew med blue print N Triangle to dk brown N Triangle; sew blue/gray H Triangle to units just sewn, forming squares, **Fig 18**. Make four.

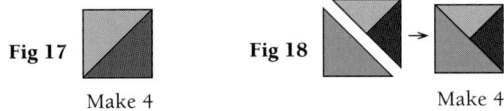

Fig 17

Make 4

Fig 18

Make 4

3. Sew med blue P Triangles on opposite sides of dk brown O Square; sew medium triangles to remaining sides forming square, **Fig 19**.

4. Arrange squares in three rows of three; sew squares in rows, then sew rows together to complete Card Trick Block, **Fig 20**.

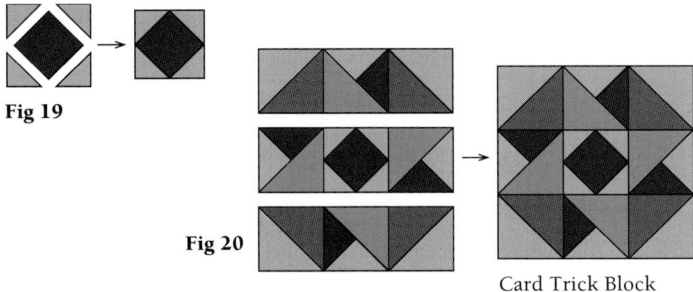

Fig 19

Fig 20

Card Trick Block

Four Patch Block

1. Sew a striped G Triangle to a dk brown G Triangle to form a square, **Fig 21**. Make 2.

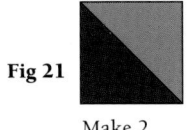

Fig 21

Make 2

2. Sew brown solid 2" square to a dk blue 2" square; repeat. Sew pairs of squares to form four patch unit, **Fig 22**. Make 2.

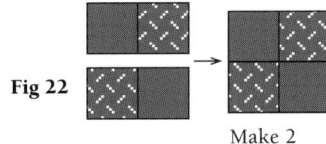

Fig 22

Make 2

3. Sew triangle units to four patch units; repeat. Sew rows to complete Four Patch Block, **Fig 23**.

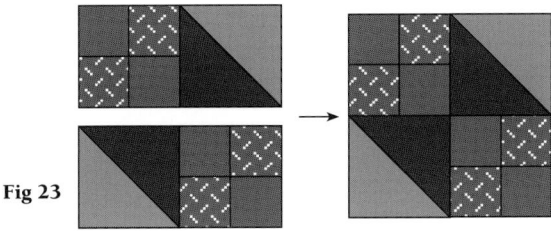

Fig 23

Four Patch Block

Finishing

1. Place blocks, sashing strips and setting squares according to layout. Sew blocks to sashing strips; then sew sashing strips to setting squares. Sew all rows together.

2. Layer and baste.

3. Quilt as desired. Photographed quilt was tied in corners using perle cotton.

4. Trim batting and lining to match quilt top.

5. Piece binding strips so that the lt brown strips are at the corners bordered by lt brown sashing. (Refer to color photograph on back cover for placement.) Attach binding following instructions on page 6.

6. Sign and date your quilt.

Quilt Layout

33

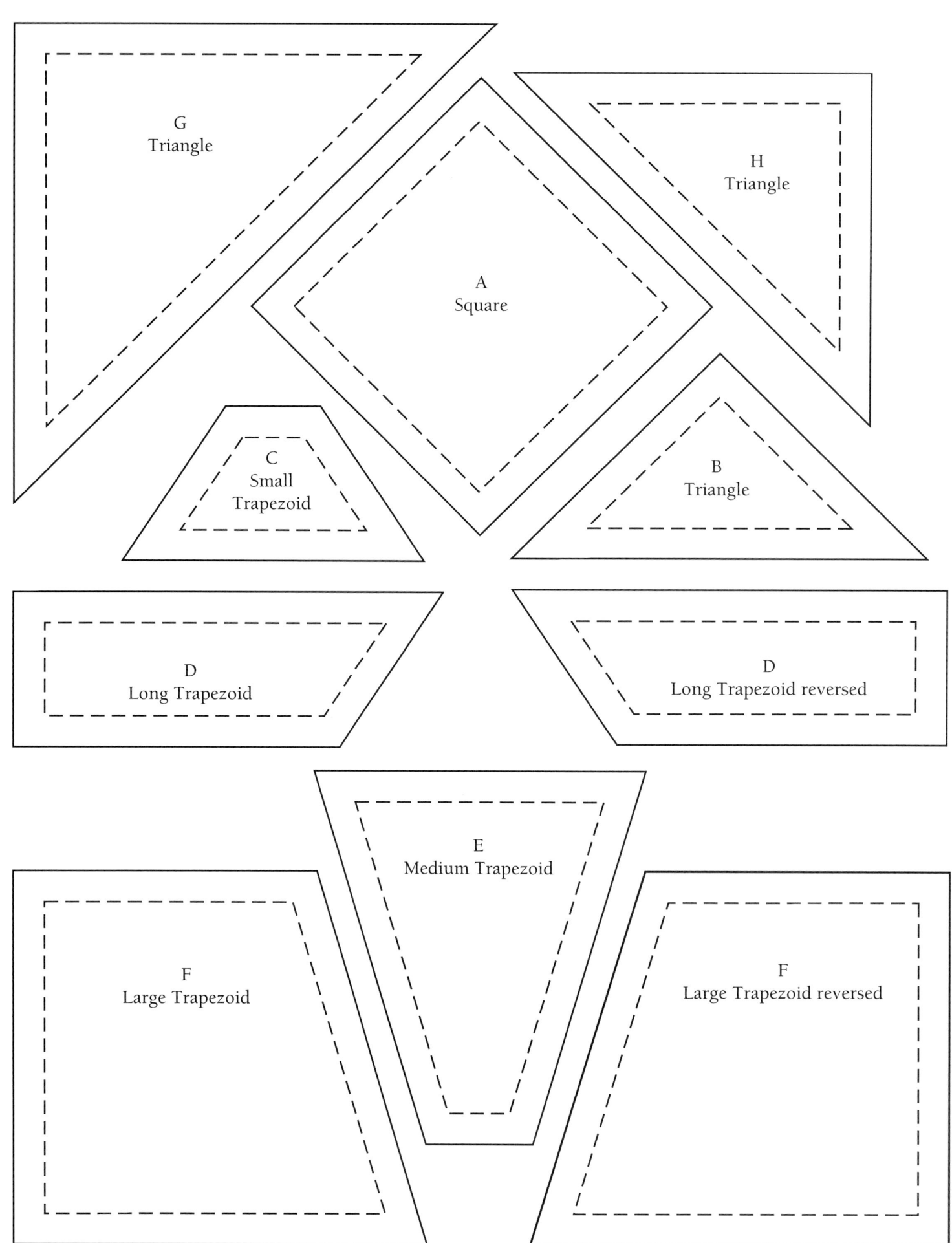

G
Triangle

H
Triangle

A
Square

C
Small
Trapezoid

B
Triangle

D
Long Trapezoid

D
Long Trapezoid reversed

E
Medium Trapezoid

F
Large Trapezoid

F
Large Trapezoid reversed

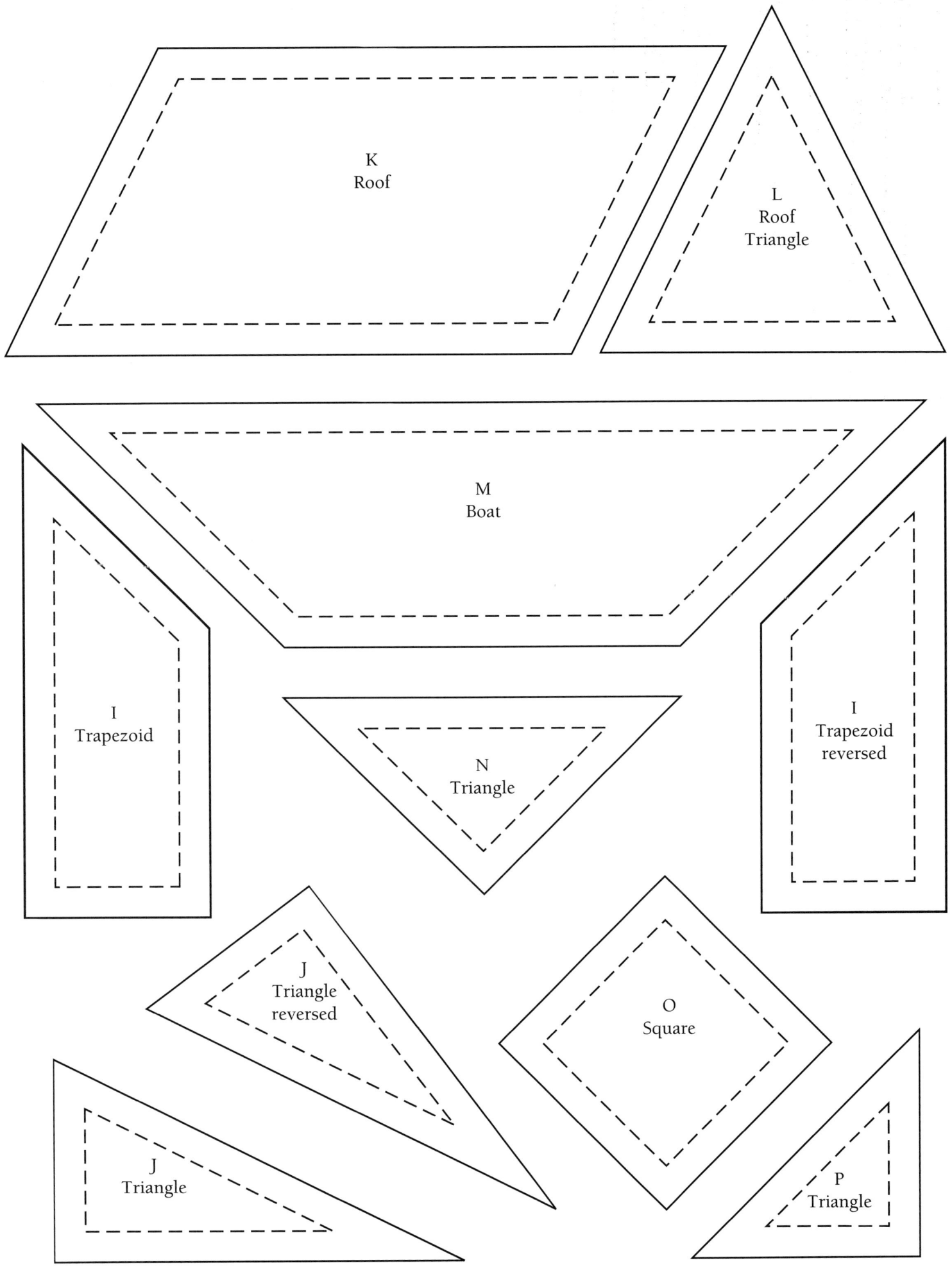

K
Roof

L
Roof
Triangle

M
Boat

I
Trapezoid

I
Trapezoid
reversed

N
Triangle

J
Triangle
reversed

O
Square

J
Triangle

P
Triangle

Joel's Star

Sharon Newman of Lubbock, Texas made this small quilt in 1995. Ties were chosen in a limited color range.

Wall Quilt: 28" x 24"

Fabric Requirements:

15 to 20 ties in light, medium, and dark tones
3/4 yd lining
batting

Pattern Pieces:

4" Blocks

A Triangle
B Triangle
C Triangle
D Square
E Square
F Triangle
G Square
H Square
I Triangle

Star Block

J Triangle
K Square
L Triangle
M Triangle
N Triangle
O Square

Cutting Requirements:

Star Block

one O Square, dk gray tie
four O Squares, lt gray tie
eight N Triangles, dk burgundy tie
four M Triangles, lt gray tie
four K Squares, dk gray tie
eight L Triangles, med burgundy tie
four J Triangles, dk gray tie

4" Blocks

five A Triangles, med burgundy tie
five A Triangles, dk burgundy tie
two A Triangles, med gray tie
two A Triangles, dk gray tie
two B Triangles, dk burgundy tie
two B Triangles, lt gray tie
four C Triangles, dk burgundy tie
two C Triangles, dk gray tie
six C Triangles, lt gray tie
one D Square, dk burgundy tie
one D Square, med gray tie
two E Squares, med gray tie

Shown in color on page 23

two E Squares, dk burgundy tie
eight F Right Triangles, dk burgundy tie
twelve F Right Triangles, med gray tie
eight G Squares, dk burgundy tie
six G Squares, dk gray tie
four H Squares, med gray tie
four H Squares, dk burgundy tie
five I Triangles, dk burgundy tie
four I Triangles, med gray tie

	Med Burgundy
	Dk Grey
	Dk Burgundy
	Lt Grey
	Med Grey

Border

twelve 2 1/2" x 4 1/2" rectangles, burgundy tie
twelve 2 1/2" x 4 1/2" rectangles, gray tie

Binding

1 1/2"-wide bias strips to total about 105", burgundy ties

Sewing Instructions:

Star Block

1. For small star, sew a med burgundy L Triangle to each diagonal edge of dk gray J Triangle, **Fig 1**. Make 4.

2. Sew a dk gray K Square to each short end of one unit just made, **Fig 2**. Repeat for second unit.

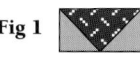 Fig 1    Fig 2

3. Sew remaining pieced units from step 1 to opposite sides of dk gray O Square, **Fig 3**. Sew units from step 2 to top and bottom to complete small star, **Fig 4**.

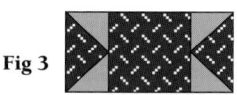 Fig 3

 Fig 4

4. Sew dk burgundy N Triangles to diagonal edges of lt gray M Triangle, **Fig 5**. Make 4.

5. Sew a lt gray O Square to each short end of one unit just made, **Fig 6**. Repeat for second unit.

6. Sew unit from step 4 to opposite sides of small star, **Fig 7**. Sew units from step 5 to top and bottom to complete Star Block, **Fig 8**.

4" Blocks

Refer to color key and the following steps to make the ten different 4" blocks. There are twenty-one 4" blocks in all.

1. Sew med burgundy A Triangle to dk burgundy A Triangle; sew to dk burgundy I Triangle, **Fig 9**.

2. Sew dk burgundy I Triangle to med gray I Triangle, **Fig 10**. Make 4.

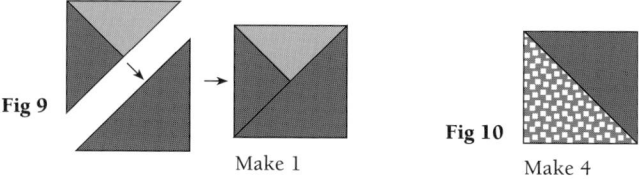

Make 1

Make 4

3. Sew med gray F Triangles to opposite sides of dk burgundy D Square; sew med gray F Triangle to remaining sides, **Fig 11**. Repeat using four dk burgundy F Triangle and one med gray D Square.

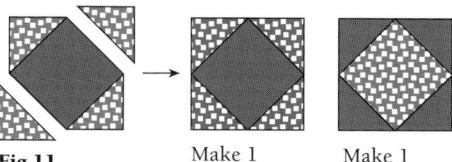

Make 1   Make 1

4. Sew med gray E Square to dk burgundy E Square; repeat. Sew pairs of squares together. Sew med gray F Triangles to opposite ends of four patch; sew med gray F Triangles to remaining sides, **Fig 12**.

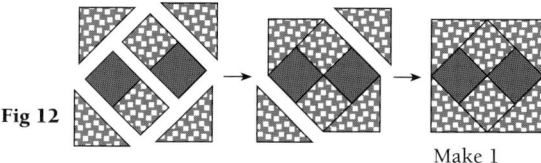

Make 1

5. Sew lt gray C Triangle to diagonal edges of dk burgundy B Triangle, **Fig 13**; repeat. Make two more blocks using a lt gray B Triangle and two dk burgundy C Triangles for each.

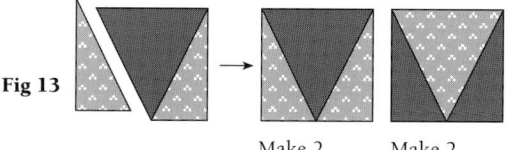

Make 2   Make 2

6. Sew dk burgundy F Triangle to med gray F Triangle; repeat 3 more times. Sew together to complete block, **Fig 14.**

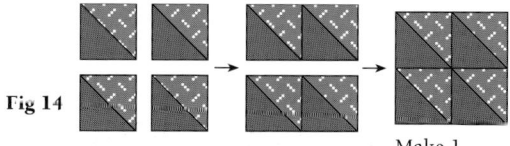

Make 1

7. Sew dk gray G Square to dk burgundy G Square; repeat. Sew pairs together to complete block, **Fig 15**. Make 3.

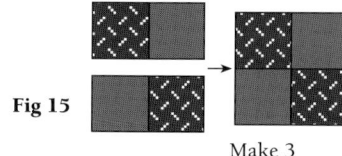

Make 3

8. Sew med gray H Square to dk burgundy H Square; repeat 3 more times. Sew 2 pairs together to form four patch; repeat. Sew four patch to dk burgundy G Square; repeat. Sew halves to complete block, **Fig 16**.

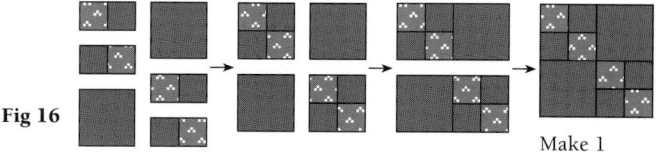

Make 1

9. Sew dk gray A Triangle to dk burgundy A Triangle; repeat. Sew pairs together, **Fig 17**. Repeat using two dk burgundy A Triangles and two med gray A Triangles for one block and two med gray A Triangles and two med burgundy A Triangles for another.

Make 1   Make 1   Make 1

10. Sew dk burgundy C Triangle to lt gray C Triangle; repeat. Sew pairs together to complete block, **Fig 18**.

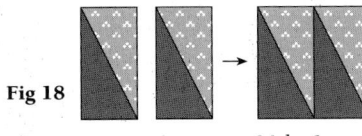

Fig 18

Make 1

Finishing:

1. Arrange 4" squares around Star Block following Quilt Layout.

2. Sew blocks together in rows around Star Block; then sew rows to Star Block, **Fig 19**.

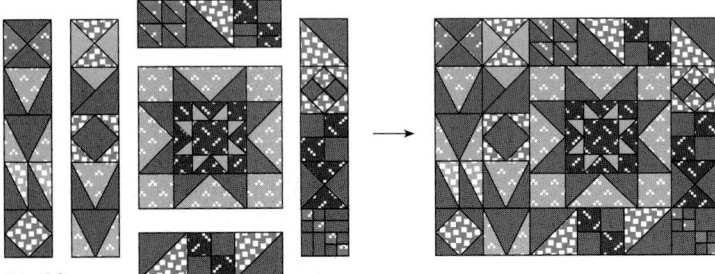

Fig 19

3. For side border, sew three gray rectangles and two burgundy rectangles end to end; repeat. Sew to each side.

4. For top border, sew four burgundy rectangles and three gray rectangles end to end; repeat for bottom. Sew to top and bottom of quilt.

5. Layer and baste.

6. Make invisible tailor tacks at seam lines and intersections about every four inches.

7. Trim batting and lining to match quilt top.

8. Bind.

9. Sign and date your quilt.

Quilt Layout

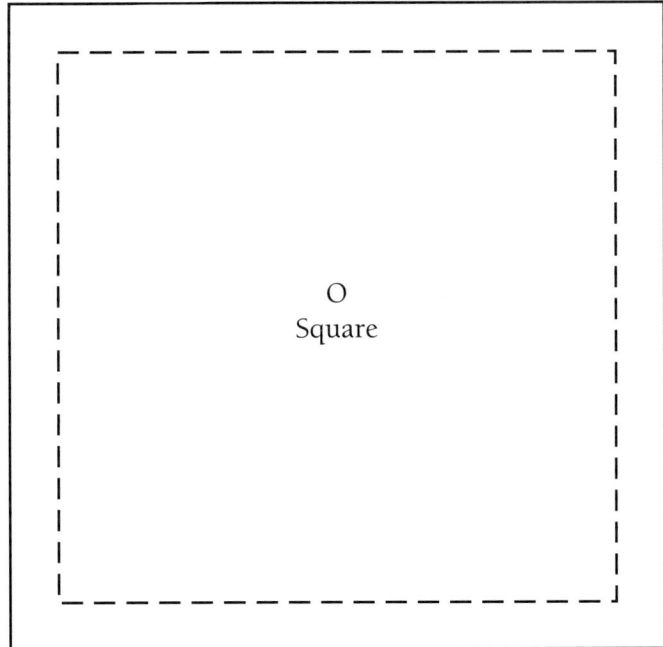

O
Square

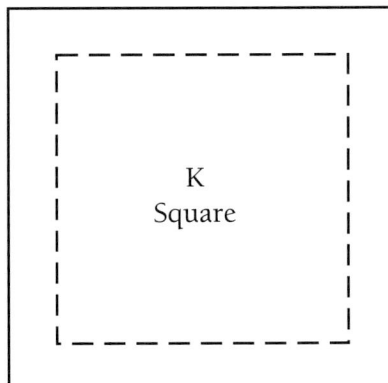

K
Square

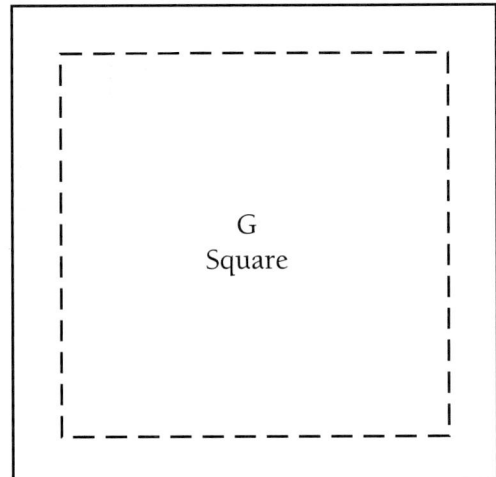

G
Square

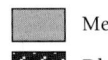 Med Burgundy

 Dk Grey

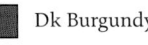 Dk Burgundy

 Lt Grey

 Med Grey

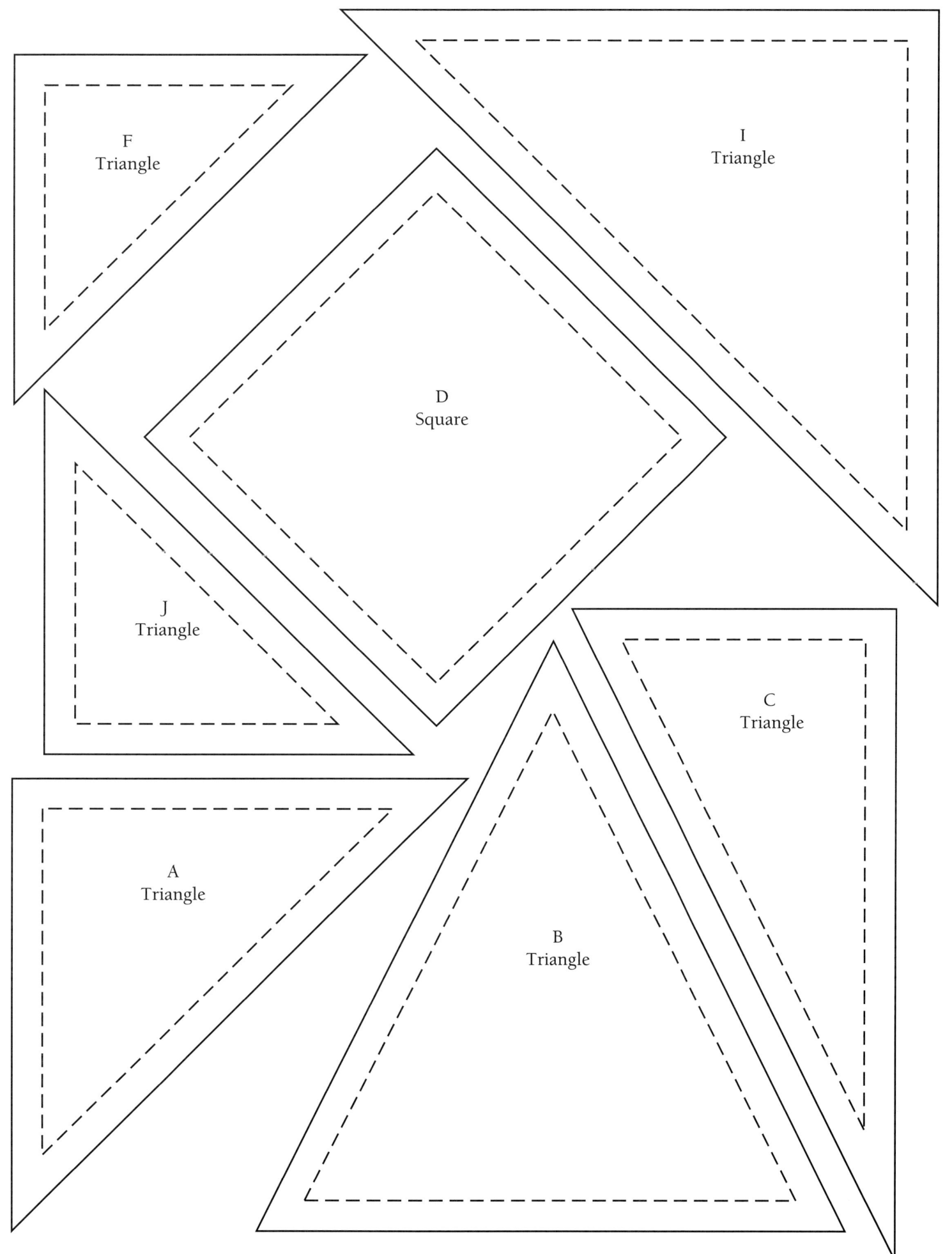

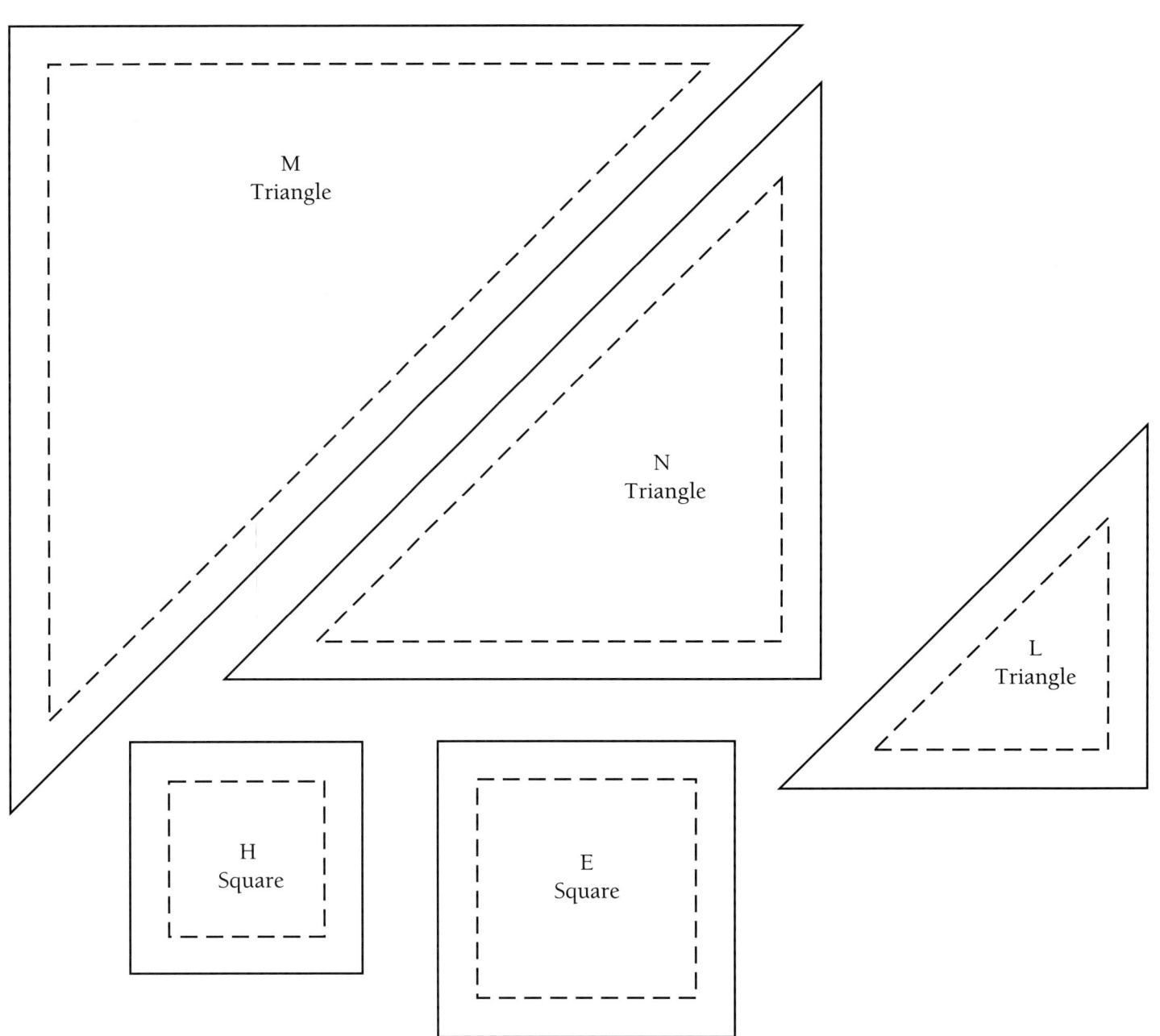

M
Triangle

N
Triangle

L
Triangle

H
Square

E
Square

Tessellating Ties

Barbara Thorne designed and made this original Log Cabin variation quilt using fabrics from men's ties. She chose to use only gray neutrals accented with red. Friends helped her collect enough ties in the chosen colors to complete the quilt. Tessellating Ties was juried into the 1994 American Quilter's Society exhibit.

Wall Quilt: 56" x 64 1/2"

Fabric Requirements:

35 to 50 ties (light, medium, and dark gray, with black and red for accents)
5 yds muslin for foundations
1 yd lt gray solid for centers and outline border
1/2 yd med gray solid for border
2 yds black solid for border and binding
3 1/2 yds fabric for lining
batting

Additional Supplies:

Roll of paper such as shelf paper, butcher paper or newsprint

Pattern Pieces:

A Foundation Shape
B Center Shape

Cutting List:

49 A Foundation Shapes, muslin
several tapered strips 3/4" to 2" wide, assorted tie fabrics
49 B Center Shapes, lt gray solid
26 strips, 1 3/4"-wide x length of outside blocks*, lt gray solid
two 1 3/4" x 52" strips, med gray solid
two 1 3/4" x 60" strips, med gray solid
two 3" x 58" strips, black solid
two 4" x 66" strips, black solid
*These are cut to length after sewing the blocks. See steps 2 through 6 of Border and Finishing instructions.

Sewing Instructions:

Making the Block

Note: *Press tie fabric open after adding each new strip.*

1. Place gray Center Shape right side up in middle of muslin foundation, **Fig 1**. Starting on shortest side of Center Shape, place a tie strip right sides together with the center gray piece. Sew with a 1/4" seam, **Fig 2**. Press strip open; trim tie strip to length of Center Shape, **Fig 3**.

Shown in color on page 23

2. Add a tie strip to opposite side of center in the same manner, **Fig 4**.

3. Add strips to remaining two sides overlapping the first strips sewn, **Fig 5**. Press and trim after adding each strip. Note that the strips are tapered randomly.

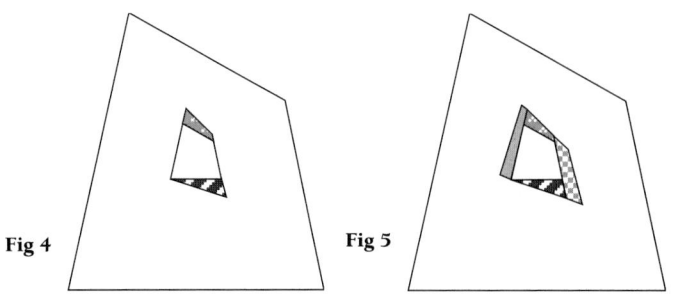

4. Working in the same order, add strips to cover Foundation Shape completely, **Fig 6**.

5. Trim overlapping tie fabric even with Foundation Shape, **Fig 7**.

6. Zigzag stitch on the outer edge of Foundation Shape stabilizing the last row added, **Fig 8**.

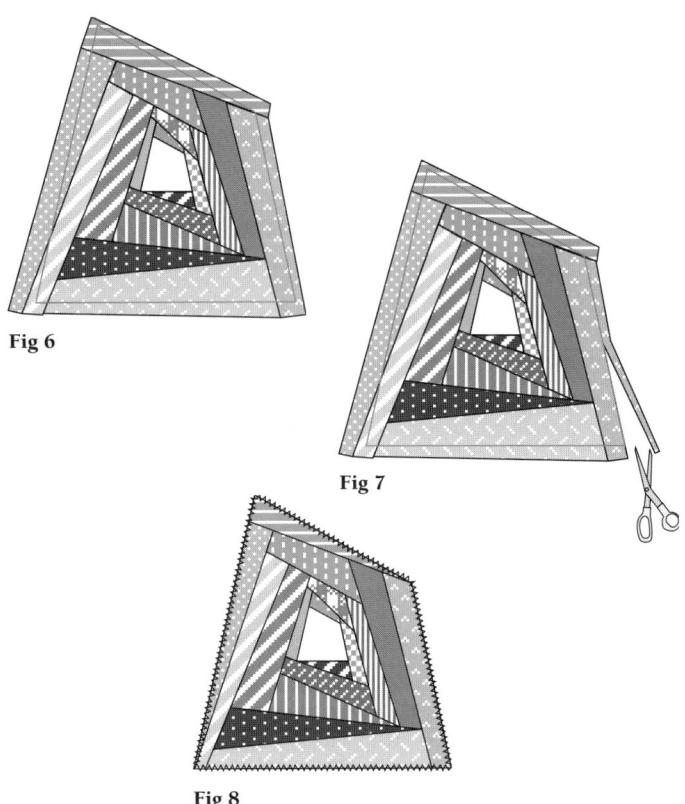

Fig 6

Fig 7

Fig 8

7. Repeat steps 1 to 6 for a total of 49 blocks.

Borders and Finishing:

1. Arrange finished blocks with seven across and seven down, rotating the shapes so they fit together smoothly, **Fig 9**. When the arrangement is satisfactory, make an outline of each side on large piece of paper (tape pieces of paper together if necessary).

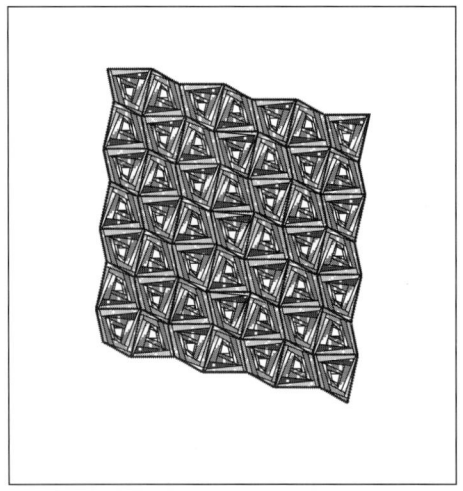

Fig 9

2. Draw a line 1 1/4" outside of first line for lt gray border; also, draw lines in border to show where blocks meet, **Fig 10**.

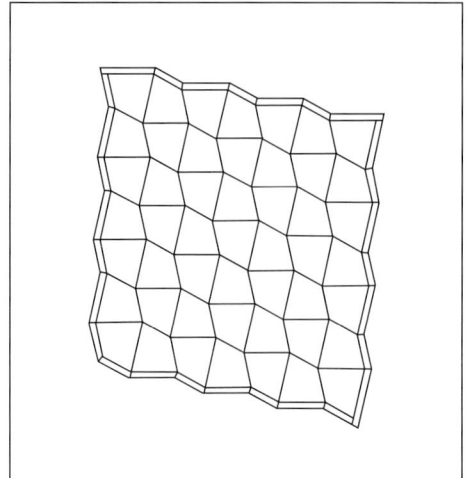

Fig 10

3. Use a long straight-edge and mark the paper forming a rectangle for pieced border beyond the light gray border, **Fig 11**. Note that lower right corner extends below drawn line.

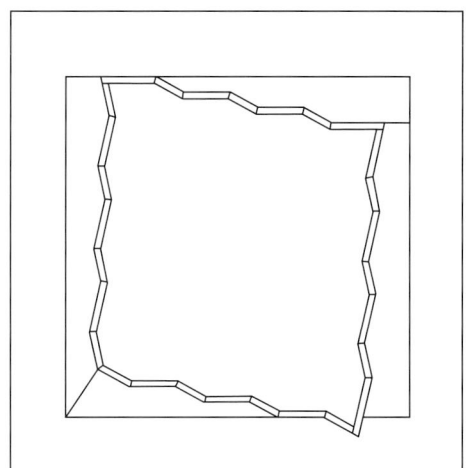

Fig 11

4. Draw a line 1 1/4" from outside edge of line just drawn for med gray border, **Fig 12**.

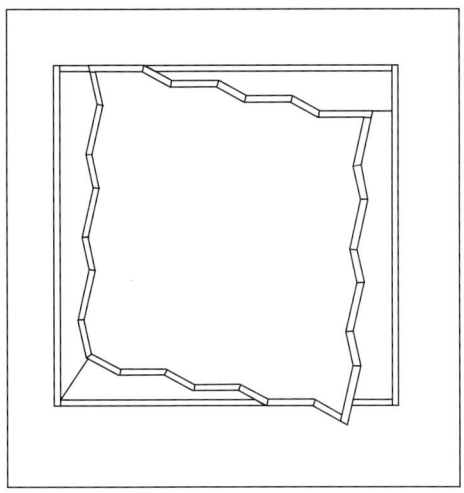

Fig 12

5. Cut out drawn pattern pieces for lt gray border, pieced border and med gray border. ***Note:*** *Be sure to keep pieces in order.*

6. Cut border pieces from lt gray fabric, adding 1/4" seam allowance around; stitch each piece to its corresponding shape, **Fig 13**. ***Note:*** *Corner blocks have two lt gray border pieces.*

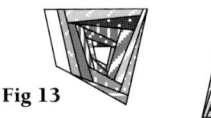

Fig 13

7. Stitch the blocks together. ***Note:*** *The light gray border will be completed as the shapes are joined.*

8. Make muslin foundations for the four pieced sections of border; be sure to add 1/4" seam allowance all around when cutting out.

9. Cover the pieced border foundations using strips of tie fabric. Start in the center of each foundation and add pieces on both sides, **Fig 14**. Continue until entire foundation is covered. Trim edges even with muslin foundation.

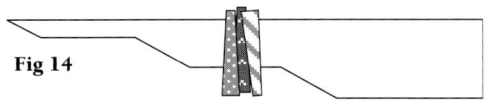

Fig 14

10. Cut med gray border strips using pattern pieces from step 5; be sure to add 1/4" seam allowance all around. Sew med gray border to corresponding edges of pieced border, **Fig 15**.

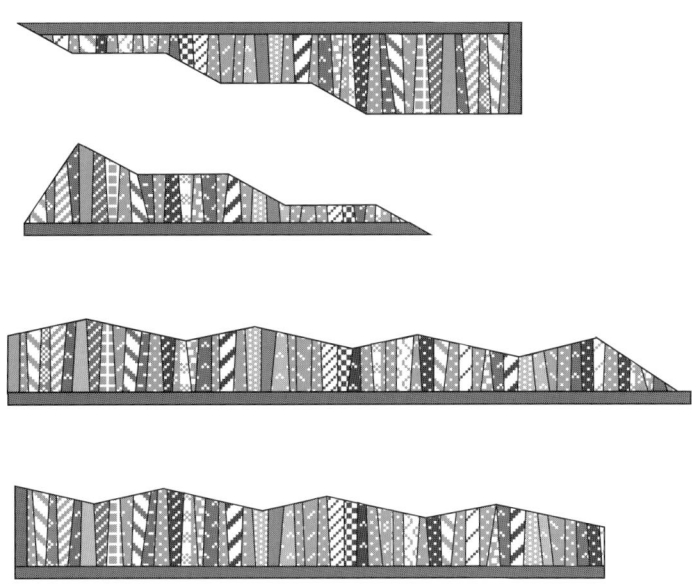

Fig 15

11. Position pieced borders around central portion of quilt. Fold raw edge of lt gray border under 1/4"; hand stitch lt gray border on top of pieced borders, **Fig 16**. Sew corner seams of pieced border.

Fig 16

12. Sew black solid border to sides of quilt.

13. Sew black solid border to top edge of quilt. Sew black solid border to bottom edge of quilt, stopping at folded lt gray border where block overlaps; continue stitching on other side of overlap, **Fig 17**. Fold black border open; press. Bring overlapped block on top of black border; hand stitch light gray border edge in place on lower border, **Fig 18**.

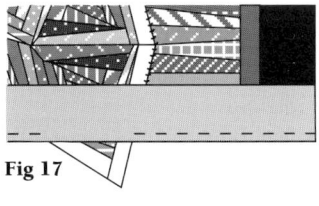

Fig 17

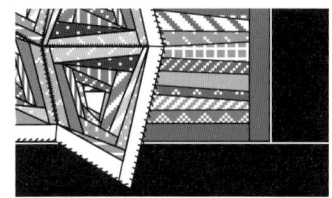

Fig 18

14. Mark for quilting.

15. Layer and baste.

16. Quilt and bind.

17. Sign and date your quilt.

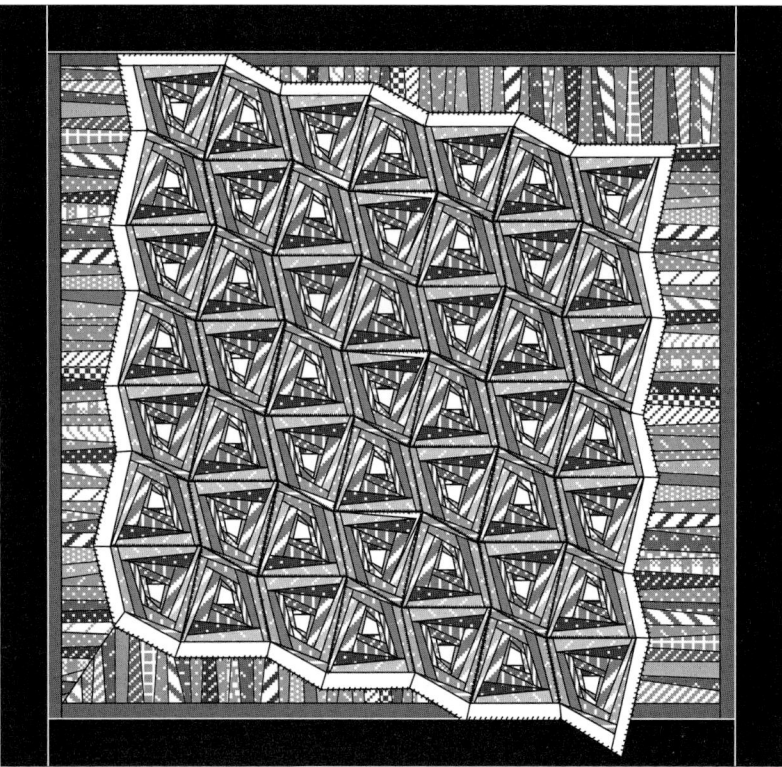

Quilt Layout